T0194770

ABOUT THE AUTHOR OF THE ORIGINAL WORK

Gordon Allport (1897–1967) was born in Indiana in the United States. He studied at Harvard University, and went on to work there for 40 years. He made huge contributions to the field of personality psychology and his influence is still felt today. Allport lived through important and unsettling historical times, including the Holocaust and the American Civil Rights Movement. This gave him a burning desire to tap into psychological explanations for the violent, discriminatory behavior of so many people. He was convinced that social science had a vital role to play in giving governments policy guidance to reduce the evil of discrimination.

ABOUT THE AUTHORS OF THE ANALYSIS

Dr Alexander O'Connor did his postgraduate work at the University of California, Berkeley, where he received a PhD for work on social and personality psychology.

ABOUT MACAT

GREAT WORKS FOR CRITICAL THINKING

Macat is focused on making the ideas of the world's great thinkers accessible and comprehensible to everybody, everywhere, in ways that promote the development of enhanced critical thinking skills.

It works with leading academics from the world's top universities to produce new analyses that focus on the ideas and the impact of the most influential works ever written across a wide variety of academic disciplines. Each of the works that sit at the heart of its growing library is an enduring example of great thinking. But by setting them in context – and looking at the influences that shaped their authors, as well as the responses they provoked – Macat encourages readers to look at these classics and game-changers with fresh eyes. Readers learn to think, engage and challenge their ideas, rather than simply accepting them.

'Macat offers an amazing first-of-its-kind tool for interdisciplinary learning and research. Its focus on works that transformed their disciplines and its rigorous approach, drawing on the world's leading experts and educational institutions, opens up a world-class education to anyone.'

Andreas Schleicher,
Director for Education and Skills, Organisation for Economic
Co-operation and Development

'Macat is taking on some of the major challenges in university education … They have drawn together a strong team of active academics who are producing teaching materials that are novel in the breadth of their approach.'

Prof Lord Broers,
former Vice-Chancellor of the University of Cambridge

'The Macat vision is exceptionally exciting. It focuses upon new modes of learning which analyse and explain seminal texts which have profoundly influenced world thinking and so social and economic development. It promotes the kind of critical thinking which is essential for any society and economy.
This is the learning of the future.'

Rt Hon Charles Clarke, former UK Secretary of State for Education

'The Macat analyses provide immediate access to the critical conversation surrounding the books that have shaped their respective discipline, which will make them an invaluable resource to all of those, students and teachers, working in the field.'

Professor William Tronzo, University of California at San Diego

WAYS IN TO THE TEXT

KEY POINTS

- Gordon Allport was an American psychologist who had a profound and lasting impact on his field.
- *The Nature of Prejudice* gives a comprehensive understanding of the psychology of prejudice, explaining how and why prejudice exists.
- The ideas that Allport put forward in *The Nature of Prejudice* shaped the study of prejudice for decades and are still relevant today.

Who was Gordon Allport?

Gordon Willard Allport (1897–1967) was born in Montezuma, Indiana, the youngest of four sons. One of his elder brothers, Floyd Henry Allport,* was an influential social psychologist* himself and played a key role in developing Gordon's career. Floyd studied psychology at the prestigious Harvard University and encouraged Gordon to enroll there as an undergraduate. The two brothers later went on to collaborate on a book on personality psychology.*

After gaining his degree in philosophy and economics in 1919, Allport headed for Europe, teaching in Istanbul, Turkey, for a period. He also visited Sigmund Freud*—who became known as the father of psychoanalytic therapy*—in Vienna in 1920. Allport returned to Harvard that same year to begin a PhD in psychology, earning his doctorate in 1922. The university then awarded Allport a traveling fellowship, and he returned to Europe to study Gestalt psychology* in Berlin and Hamburg. This new school of psychology placed particular emphasis on the cognitive* (or conscious thought). The experience shaped Allport's later work and influenced his move toward the use of cognitive theory rather than psychodynamic* or behaviorist* thinking.

Allport returned to Harvard University in 1924, where he worked first as an instructor and then as a professor for the best part of four decades until his death in 1967. He was elected president of the American Psychological Association in 1939.

Published in 1954, Allport's fourth book, *The Nature of Prejudice*, is his best-known work and is considered one of the most important and influential texts in social psychology. Allport is also known as one of the founders of personality psychology and wrote a number of books on the subject, including the influential *Becoming: Basic Considerations for Psychology of Personality* in 1955.

What Does *The Nature Of Prejudice* Say?

Allport wanted to integrate already-existing research on prejudice* with his own ideas to show that:

- prejudice is widespread
- prejudice does not have a single cause, but is the result of many different factors
- prejudice and discrimination can be limited and, ultimately, combated.

Decades of research have followed *The Nature of Prejudice*, but the majority of Allport's conclusions stand up today, and the original ideas he explained in the book are still relevant. Allport's highly influential intergroup contact hypothesis* was first outlined here. This hypothesis suggests that if people have increased experience of a group outside their own, then their attitudes toward that group will improve.

With *The Nature of Prejudice*, Allport changed the focus of personality psychology. The Freudian analytic approach, in which a person's childhood experiences are thought to shape his or her unconscious and forge the personality, had some support. At the time the book was published in 1954, behaviorism was the approach that dominated. Behaviorism puts forward the idea that we are all effectively blank slates and that our character traits* are created by external, environmental factors. Allport looked at both the Freudian and behaviorist approaches, and considered both to be too extreme. Freud's psychodynamic approach didn't seem to recognize the importance of conscious thought (the cognitive), while behaviorism appeared to deny the importance that thought processes and experience, whether conscious or unconscious, could have on someone's personality. Allport expressed his support for a more cognitive approach, suggesting that personality is formed by conscious mental activities such as attitudes, beliefs, and memory processing. This was a significant shift in the field of psychology, and Allport's work in *The Nature of Prejudice* helped develop the field of social cognition.*

Allport argues in his book that prejudice has many causes and that all human beings are capable of it. His theory suggests that prejudice is the result of cognitive processes, of patterns of thinking and beliefs. One of these cognitive processes, the "least-effort principle,"* was described by Allport before anyone else in relation to prejudice. In the least-effort principle, a person uses generalizations and stereotypes* as a mental shortcut to form a view of someone, rather than taking the longer route, drawing on memory and judgment. Allport said that these stereotypes, or shortcuts, are often based on visible features, such as a person's race.

Allport's intention in writing *The Nature of Prejudice* was to make a positive difference, as prejudice and discrimination were widespread in the United States and the rest of the world. The book was written when the shocking details of the Holocaust* had recently become known and the American Civil Rights Movement,* which was fighting for greater rights for minority groups, was gaining momentum. *The Nature of Prejudice* developed new ideas, but also offered a comprehensive look at all the existing theories on the subject. Allport found the idea of behaviorism negative, because it put forward the notion that change could come about only through a modification in the environment in which people were living. So in this framework the only way it would be possible to change prejudice would be to alter the poor economic situations in which certain groups lived. Allport suggested that how people think about things—cognition— was a much more significant factor in conquering prejudice. He believed that once it was better understood *why* prejudice occurred, social scientists would then be moved to act to influence policy-makers to curb discrimination by political means. *The Nature of Prejudice* was widely read and admired when it was first published, and some anti-discrimination laws were indeed introduced in the years after it appeared. It could be concluded that Allport's ideas in *The Nature of Prejudice* had some influence in reducing prejudice and discrimination. There is little hard evidence of a direct link, however, so it is not possible to say exactly *how much* social change Allport's psychological investigation of prejudice concretely achieved.

Why Does *The Nature Of Prejudice* Matter?

The Nature of Prejudice is essential reading for anyone interested in personality and psychology. In 2005, a collection of essays to mark the 50th anniversary of the book was published. Called *On the Nature of Prejudice: Fifty Years after Allport*, each essay paid tribute to Allport's core themes. Written by the most influential prejudice researchers working in psychology—such as John Dovidio* and Susan Fiske*—the essays give credit to Allport for paving the way for most contemporary social psychological research on prejudice. In his introduction, Dovidio says, "There is no debate that Gordon Allport's (1954/1979) *The Nature of Prejudice* is the foundational work for the social psychology of prejudice. Contemporary prejudice researchers and scholars regularly refer back to this work not only for apt quotations, but also for inspiration. Social science instructors often pair Allport's book with recent articles. Indeed, any student of prejudice ignorant of Allport would be rightly considered illiterate."[1]

The Nature of Prejudice is also invaluable reading for anyone interested in the growth of the human rights movements of the mid-twentieth century. In particular, Allport's ideas about prejudice act as a historical record of the early times of the American Civil Rights Movement. This is because his ideas represent the central arguments that were put forward by the movement, aiming to reduce prejudice and discrimination and improve the rights of minority groups. In addition, the book also supported and informed legislation intended to fight discrimination in the United States. Allport believed that "legislation, if enforced, may be a sharp tool in the battle against discrimination."[2]

Finally, Allport gave balanced consideration to many different theories of prejudice. He drew from most areas of psychology, including clinical,* social, personality, and developmental* psychology. Not only does *The Nature of Prejudice* provide an introduction to the broader field of psychology, it also emphasizes that most psychological phenomena are determined by a number of different factors.

NOTES

1   John F. Dovidio et al., *On the Nature of Prejudice: Fifty Years after Allport* (Abingdon: Blackwell Publishing, 2005), 1.

2   Gordon W. Allport, *The Nature of Prejudice* (New York: Basic Books, 1979), 442.

SECTION 1
INFLUENCES

MODULE 1
THE AUTHOR AND THE HISTORICAL CONTEXT

KEY POINTS

- Several modern theories of prejudice,* such as the intergroup contact theory,* have their origins in *The Nature of Prejudice.*
- Allport was a leading personality psychologist,* and his examination of the causes of prejudice led to the cognitive revolution.*
- He was influenced by world events of the 1940s and 1950s: World War II,* the Holocaust,* and the American Civil Rights Movement.*

Why Read this Text?

Gordon Allport's *The Nature of Prejudice* is one of the most important works in the psychological study of prejudice. It has shaped the way the field of personality psychology has developed and is the text where the influential intergroup contact hypothesis was first developed. This theory suggests that if a group has more contact with members of a different race, ethnicity, gender, or religion, then the group will be less prejudiced toward those different members. The book also led the cognitive revolution and resulted in the birth of the field of social cognition.* These two movements emphasize cognitive factors (such as beliefs and memory) to explain human behavior. Until the publication of *The Nature of Prejudice*, behaviorism* had been the favored model in the field of personality psychology. In behaviorism, it is believed that a person's behavior is caused by the environment and factors *outside* the mind. After the publication of *The Nature of Prejudice*,

> ❝ Returning to Harvard in 1920, he completed his PhD in psychology in just two years. Gordon's dissertation title again reflected his dual commitment to science and social concerns: *An Experimental Study of the Traits of Personality: With Special Reference to the Problem of Social Diagnosis.* ❞
>
> Thomas F. Pettigrew,* "Gordon Willard Allport: A Tribute," *Journal of Social Issues* 55, no. 3

cognitive theory and social cognition became the most commonly used frameworks through which psychologists investigated prejudice. Intergroup contact and cognition (particularly with regard to stereotyping* and memory processes) are both areas of prejudice research that continue to be explored today. Both have their origins in Allport's book.

The Nature of Prejudice is also historically informative, because many of the ideas Allport introduces in the text reflected and supported the thinking of the American Civil Rights Movement. For example, in *The Nature of Prejudice*, Allport expressed the belief that proactive* policy—creating laws to bring about changes that are needed rather than creating laws to react to something that has already happened—was necessary for racial desegregation (that is, putting an end to the practice of separating people according to race) and improved civil rights for US minority groups. In the 1950s and 1960s, social scientists who were supportive of civil rights for all contributed to anti-discrimination and anti-segregation laws in the United States. Many of them backed up their views using evidence from *The Nature of Prejudice*. In particular, they used Allport's intergroup contact hypothesis, which supported the idea that racial desegregation would increase contact between groups and so improve intergroup relations.[1]

Author's Life

Born in Indiana in 1897, Allport was the youngest of four sons. He was raised a Christian and remained religious all his life. He dedicated a chapter in *The Nature of Prejudice* to examining the relationship between religion and prejudice.[2] Religion was the only strand of prejudice theory that Allport continued to work on after the publication of his most famous work on the subject.

Despite originally completing his BA degree in philosophy and economics, Allport was already developing an interest in psychology. While spending time in Europe in 1920 he visited the famous neurologist* Sigmund Freud* in Vienna. Nervous at meeting the man who was already gaining a reputation as a "father of psychology," the young Allport tried to break the ice by telling Freud a story about how he had seen a boy on the train on which he was traveling to Vienna who had a phobia about dirt. Freud asked, "Was that little boy you?" Allport later wrote in an autobiographical essay that his attempt to chat with Freud had led the older man to make judgments about Allport's unconscious motivations.[3] He felt that Freud put too much emphasis on early childhood experiences and the unconscious in making these judgments. He wrote, "Freud had thought that I was suffering from an infantile trauma. I wasn't. If he had said I was a brassy young American, he would have been right. But, he didn't … I don't deny that there may be traces of infantilism in all of us or traces of neurosis in all of us."[4] It is believed that this particular incident affected Allport's view of how personality develops. It started the process in which he put less emphasis on the role of the unconscious in developing personality and more on conscious thought or the cognitive.*

In his early academic life, Allport was influenced by the experimental psychologist Hugo Münsterberg* and by his elder brother, Floyd Henry Allport.* Floyd is considered one of the founders of the field of social psychology.*[5] Allport co-authored his first publication, *Personality Traits: Their Classification and Measurement*, with Floyd in 1921.

While working on his PhD in psychology at Harvard University, which he obtained in 1922, Allport was awarded the Sheldon Traveling Scholarship. This allowed him to spend two years studying abroad. He spent the first in Germany, where he became interested in the newly developed Gestalt psychology,* which puts an emphasis on conscious thought processes (the cognitive). He spent his second year at Cambridge University, in the UK.

Allport spent most of his academic life at Harvard University, working there for almost 40 years. He was the chair (or head) of the Psychology Department at Harvard from 1936 to 1946, at which time the department was reorganized into the Department of Social Relations. Previously, the disciplines of psychology and sociology had been clearly segregated. But this reorganization allowed for more interdisciplinary work to take place and actually led to the development of the field of social psychology.

Allport wrote *The Nature of Prejudice* in the early 1950s, during the later stages of his academic career. He said that the book "gradually took shape under the kindly stimulus of … a continuing seminar in the Department of Social Relations at Harvard."[6] This is a reference to a seminar that Allport himself taught, which he called "Group Conflict and Prejudice."

The Nature of Prejudice continues to thrive and is still relevant today. Because of the enduring impact of the book, Allport is considered the most influential researcher into prejudice and one of the founders of personality psychology. He was ranked 11th overall in a 2002 study seeking to quantify the influence of twentieth-century psychologists.[7]

Author's Background
Allport was influenced by the times in which he lived. The mid-twentieth century was an era of great social and political turmoil.

Hugely important events such as World War II, the Holocaust, and the American Civil Rights Movement forced people to think about the ways in which people and societies had developed. In the years following World War II, many social psychologists were motivated by the Holocaust. They wanted to uncover psychological explanations for these violent events. They needed to understand what had led people of different nations, ideologies, and religions to clash with such violence. One of Allport's students, the psychologist Thomas Pettigrew, described the field's interest in studying prejudice at this time: "Once Hitler* gave prejudice a bad name, the Human Relations Movement* developed after World War II to improve America's intergroup relations."[8] Allport was convinced that social science had a role to play in studying and providing government with policy suggestions to reduce discrimination and the type of genocide—the targeted destruction of a particular ethnic group—that Germany's Nazis (the far-right National Socialist party) had inflicted on the Jews.

Throughout *The Nature of Prejudice*, Allport referred to political and social events, both in the United States and around the world, to highlight real instances of prejudice. But, to him, "The checkerboard of prejudice in the United States is perhaps the most intricate of all."[9]

In the United States in the early 1950s, many of the country's southern states had *de jure* segregation.* This meant that there were actual laws in place that separated the races. Meanwhile *de facto* segregation*—where the separation of the races is not written in the law, but is the accepted way that things are done—was common in the northern states. As the American Civil Rights Movement gained momentum, racial prejudice and segregation became a topic of conversation, both politically and socially. Allport was optimistic. He thought that growing support for the civil rights movement would lead to an improvement in intergroup relations in the United States. Psychologist Irwin Katz* said, "What Allport witnessed at the time of writing his volume was the first phase in the desegregation of

American society along racial lines. Prejudice and discrimination still reigned, but signs of change were unmistakable." Katz continued, "What was yet unclear to the informed observer was how far the process of reform would go and at what pace, and this ambiguity was reflected in [Allport's] treatment of the subject."[10]

NOTES

1   Sabrina Zirkel and Nancy Cantor, "50 Years after Brown v. Board of Education: The Promise and Challenge of Multicultural Education," *Journal of Social Issues* 60, no. 1 (2004): 1–15.

2   L. A. Hjelle and D. J. Ziegler, *Personality Theories: Basic Assumptions, Research, and Applications* (New York: McGraw-Hill, 1992).

3   G. W. Allport, "Gordon W. Allport," in *History of Psychology in Autobiography*, ed. E. Boring and G. Lindsay, vol. 5 (New York: Appleton-Century-Crofts, 1967), 1–25.

4   Alan C. Elms, *Uncovering Lives: The Uneasy Alliance of Biography and Psychology* (Oxford: Oxford University Press, 1994), 79–80.

5   Daniel Katz, "Obituary: Floyd H. Allport (1890–1978)," *American Psychologist* 34 (1979): 351.

6   Gordon W. Allport, *The Nature of Prejudice* (New York: Basic Books, 1979), XIII.

7   Steven J. Haggbloom et al., "The 100 Most Eminent Psychologists of the 20th Century," *Review of General Psychology* 6, no. 2 (2002): 139–52.

8   Thomas F. Pettigrew, "Gordon Willard Allport: A Tribute," *Journal of Social Issues* 55, no. 3 (1999): 421.

9   Allport, *The Nature of Prejudice*, IX.

10 Irwin Katz, "Gordon Allport's *The Nature of Prejudice*," *Political Psychology* 12, no. 1 (1991): 129.

ACADEMIC CONTEXT

KEY POINTS

- Social psychology* seeks to understand how people's thoughts, feelings, and behaviors are affected by social situations (the presence of others).

- Behaviorism* concentrates on the relationship between outside factors and behaviors, and largely ignores emotions and cognitions. *The Nature of Prejudice* helped to shift social psychology's emphasis away from behaviorism as the most commonly used framework.

- Allport used cognitive factors as important predictors of behavior.

The Work In Its Context

The Nature of Prejudice is primarily a work of social psychology. The field of social psychology seeks to describe and predict behavior through an understanding of how people's minds are affected by their social environment. When predicting behaviors, social psychologists tend to examine three broad factors: cognitions (such as beliefs, memory processes, and ideas), emotions, and the environment (such as the temperature, number of people in a setting, and the presence of rewards and punishment). Throughout social psychology's history, social psychologists have emphasized each of these three factors differently when looking at the best way to explain behavior. During the early 1950s, when Gordon Allport was writing *The Nature of Prejudice*, the focus was on the environment's influence on behavior. By the late 1950s, the focus had shifted to the influence of the cognitive, or conscious thoughts and beliefs.

> ❝ The new Gestalt* school and its emphasis on cognition* fascinated him. Indeed, he became a partial Gestaltist, partial because he could not accept the Gestaltists' assumptions about the hard-wiring of the cognitive processes. ❞
>
> Thomas F. Pettigrew,* "Gordon Willard Allport: A Tribute," *Journal of Social Issues,* 55, no. 3

Overview of the Field

Sigmund Freud* wrote, "Psychoanalysis has always taken the view that [normal people's] fate is for the most part arranged by themselves and determined by early infantile influences."[1] Freud's belief that people are clearly shaped by their early experiences has been maintained beyond his original influence. Psychoanalysis, which is also known as "psychodynamic thought,"* therefore focuses on a person's unconscious motivations. These motivations are thought to have developed during childhood as a result of a person's early relationship with his or her parents. Although psychodynamic theory in general was less popular by the early 1950s, social scientists who believed in these psychodynamic theories still came up with ideas to explain prejudice. And these ideas proved to be popular. The most prominent psychodynamic theorist was the sociologist Theodor Adorno.* Adorno argued that the child–parent relationship could predict future prejudice. For example, if a child grew up with authoritarian (overly domineering) parents, then this could lead to future aggression and prejudice in the child.

By the early 1950s, environmental factors and their influence on behavior were being considered. B. F. Skinner,* a leading behavioral psychologist, did not believe that internal thoughts (introspection) were a cause of people's behavior. Skinner explained, "This does not mean … introspection is a kind of psychological research, nor does it mean (and this is the heart of the argument) that what are felt or introspectively observed are the causes of the behavior." Instead, he said, "An organism behaves as it does because of its current structure, but most of this is out of reach of introspection. At the moment we must content ourselves, as the methodological behaviorist insists, with a person's genetic and environment histories. What are introspectively observed are certain collateral products of those histories."[2]

Skinner was much less concerned with a person's mental processes or inner thoughts than with their surroundings and prior experiences. This system of belief was known as "psychological behaviorism."* It was the theoretical framework that was most used at the time in psychology and the social sciences. The central belief of behaviorism is that most human behavior is the result of conditioned responses. People then develop these responses through reinforcement. For example, children may clean their rooms because they have learned their parents will always reward them for doing so. Behaviorism tended to discount cognitive, emotional, and motivational states—in contrast to psychodynamic thought, which focused on emotional and motivational states. A psychodynamic theorist might say that a child who obsessively cleaned his or her room was acting due to an unconscious fear of dirt. This might have developed in response to an aspect of the child's relationship with the parents or an experience in early infancy.

Academic Influences

In the early 1920s, Allport spent a year as a visiting scholar in Berlin, Germany. There he was influenced by Gestalt psychology and particularly the Gestalt psychologist William Stern.* At that time, German Gestalt psychologists were much more interested in cognition than American psychologists. The social scientist Thomas Pettigrew, who was a student of Allport's, believed that his teacher developed an interest in cognition while in Germany. Pettigrew thought that it was because of his experiences in Germany that Allport moved away from the dominant models of behaviorism and psychodynamic thinking. Pettigrew wrote, "In social psychology, social cognition* ... veered in a largely Gestalt direction that had molded Gordon's perspective on prejudice. In short, the same influences that shaped the study of prejudice in general and stereotypes* in particular from 1960 on had earlier guided Gordon's thought."[3]

NOTES

1   Salman Akhtar and Mary Kay O'Neil, eds., *On Freud's "Beyond the Pleasure Principle"* (London: Karnac Books, 2011), 21.

2   Burrhus Frederic Skinner, *About Behaviorism* (New York: Random House, 2011).

3   Thomas F. Pettigrew, "Gordon Willard Allport: A Tribute," *Journal of Social Issues* 55, no. 3 (1999): 422.

MODULE 3
THE PROBLEM

KEY POINTS

- *The Nature of Prejudice* sought to determine the causes of the hatred, prejudice,* and genocide* that blighted the first half of the twentieth century.
- Some prejudice researchers sought to compare the performances, abilities, and traits* of people of different ethnicities. Others tended to concentrate on personality as the origins of prejudice.
- Allport focused on the cognitive* influences of prejudice.

Core Question

The Nature of Prejudice was written by Gordon Allport in the early to mid-1950s, when racial, ethnic, and religious prejudices had been proved to be very harmful. Yet social psychologists* had not reached agreement as to how or why prejudices between different groups existed. Allport tried to understand what it was that drove these different racial and ethnic groups apart. Like many social scientists of the time, he was particularly interested in the causes of anti-Semitism (prejudice against Jews) after details of the Holocaust* emerged. Allport wrote *The Nature of Prejudice* to try to work out the psychological reasons behind conflicts such as World War II,* the Holocaust, and the Jim Crow laws* in the United States. These conflicts between people of different religions, races, and nationalities led social psychologists to question the causes of hatred, prejudice, and intergroup violence. And racial and ethnic prejudice also became more a part of the national conversation in the United States as the American Civil Rights Movement* gained momentum in the early 1950s.

> ❝ Civilized men have gained notable mastery over energy, matter, inanimate nature generally, and are rapidly learning to control physical suffering and premature death. But, by contrast, we appear to be living in the Stone Age so far as our handling of human relationships is concerned. ❞
>
> Gordon W. Allport, *The Nature of Prejudice*

The Participants

Before the publication of *The Nature of Prejudice*, there were two main approaches to the study of prejudice. The first focused on intergroup relations descriptively. This means that researchers set out to record and describe the actual differences that occurred in different groups such as racial, ethnic, cultural, and gender groups. They carried out tests and documented the differences in various performance and personality measures.[1] One of the best known of these studies was of newborn infants of different races conducted by the psychiatrist Benjamin Pasamanick* in the 1940s. He wanted to discover if the babies had any heritable (inborn) racial differences *before* they had been influenced by their environment.

While Pasamanick focused on babies, others tested different age groups. It was, for example, common to use intelligence quotient (IQ)* tests to try to identify real differences between different racial and ethnic groups. The idea was that if such differences existed, then stereotypes* might be based on something real. However, in the years before Allport wrote *The Nature of Prejudice*, psychologists had begun to question how real such differences actually were. They also cast doubt on the extent to which any differences found were genetic or innate group differences.[2] Or, again, whether any differences were actually a result of environmental factors, such as social, educational, economic, psychological, or cultural differences.

Psychodynamics* was the second of the two main approaches to the study of prejudice used by social psychologists to study prejudice. The sociologist Theodor Adorno* was the best-known academic to use a psychodynamic framework. Adorno and his collaborators put forward the idea that prejudice was the result of a personality type—the "authoritarian" personality. To summarize this, the social psychologist Irwin Katz* wrote, "Adorno et al ... proposed that bigotry [intolerance] was a component of a more general anti-democratic ideology commonly found in personalities marked by cognitive rigidity, repressed affect,* and self-alienation.* Supposedly, this structure was a product of punitive and autocratic [dictatorial] childrearing practices."[3]

The Contemporary Debate

The early 1950s saw the earliest stages of decline in the field's dominant framework—psychological behaviorism.* The focus on the environment as the cause of behavior meant that there was little consideration of the cognitive processes involved. According to Thomas Pettigrew,* Allport "assumed the role of counterpuncher against prevailing dogmas."[4] The cognitive influences on prejudice were generally neglected, but Allport highlighted them in *The Nature of Prejudice*. He also wrote about the value of applying more general work on cognition to the study of prejudice: "One of the most important psychological discoveries of recent years," he said in *The Nature of Prejudice*, "is that the dynamics of prejudice tend to parallel the dynamics of cognition ... the style of thinking that is characteristic of prejudice is a reflection, by and large, of the prejudiced person's way of thinking about anything."[5]

Allport had a complicated relationship with behaviorism. While he rejected most of its ideas, he did accept at least one behaviorist explanation of prejudice. Allport agreed that prejudice could be established through repeated negative experiences of a different group.

However, in Allport's view this did not explain the whole phenomenon of prejudice.

Freudian psychodynamics had much less influence by 1950, but psychodynamic theories of prejudice remained popular. These theories stated that prejudice is the result of aggressive and authoritarian* tendencies developed during childhood. Allport accepted the view that aggression can be irrationally directed at members of another group because the members of that group are an easy target. He did not agree, however, that this was a common factor leading to prejudice, and he did not think that psychodynamic theories of aggression could be used as a comprehensive theory of prejudice. Allport dedicated a chapter of *The Nature of Prejudice* to proving as much. Pettigrew wrote, "Instead of the psychodynamic steam boiler model of aggression and catharsis,* Gordon proposed a feedback model … aggression, Gordon argued, feeds on itself. That is, the acting out of aggression, rather than leading to less aggression, actually increases the probability that further aggression will be expressed."[6]

NOTES

1   Nathaniel David Mttron Hirsch, *A Study of Natio-racial Mental Differences, Genetic Psychology Monographs* (Worcester, MA: Clark University, 1926).

2   Benjamin Pasamanick, "A Comparative Study of the Behavioral Development of Negro Infants," *The Pedagogical Seminary and Journal of Genetic Psychology* 69, no. 1 (1946): 3–44.

3   Irwin Katz, "Gordon Allport's *The Nature of Prejudice*," *Political Psychology* 12, no. 1 (1991): 130.

4   Thomas F. Pettigrew, "Gordon Willard Allport: A Tribute," *Journal of Social Issues* 55, no. 3 (1999): 421.

5   Gordon W. Allport, *The Nature of Prejudice* (New York: Basic Books, 1979), 376–7.

6   Pettigrew, "Gordon Willard Allport," 421.

THE AUTHOR'S CONTRIBUTION

KEY POINTS

- Allport believed that prejudice* did not result from any single cause, but that there are many different causes of prejudice.

- Allport's argument that cognitive* factors, such as stereotyping,* are particularly influential in the formation of prejudice led to the cognitive framework becoming the most commonly used in the field.

- Allport was inspired by cognitive scientists and their explanations of behavior such as the "least-effort principle."*

Author's Aims

In *The Nature of Prejudice*, Gordon Allport wanted to provide a comprehensive analysis of how and why prejudice exists. To do this he set out to integrate all the existing social and psychological research on prejudice. He wrote, "It is a serious error to ascribe prejudice and discrimination to any single taproot, reaching into economic exploitation, social structures, the mores, fear, aggression, sex conflict, or any other favored soil. Prejudice and discrimination, as we shall see, may draw nourishment from all these conditions, and many others."[1]

Allport examined all possible theories, but he focused most on cognitive factors as a cause of prejudice. For example, he stated that stereotyping is actually a normal process used by the brain to store and process information. At the time, such cognitive factors were not being considered very closely by other psychologists examining prejudice, which made Allport's work unique. But what was also unique about *The Nature of Prejudice* was the way Allport wrote for specifically

> ❝ We may lay it down as a general law applying to all social phenomena that multiple causation* is invariably at work and nowhere is the law more clearly applicable than to prejudice. ❞
>
> Gordon W. Allport, *The Nature of Prejudice*

intended audiences. The groups of people he most wanted to reach were American citizens (specifically, white Protestant* males, because they were the largest group with power), social scientists, and the world's politicians and lawmakers. For each of those three groups, Allport wrote a series of specially tailored passages.

Approach

Allport argued that the development of prejudice is caused by many factors, such as social and cultural issues, actual differences between groups, and cognitive processes that rely on categorizing information. He considered each of those factors helpful in examining prejudice, and he was the first in the field to think in a balanced way about the many different elements that produce prejudice. Because he believed that prejudice was the result of many different causes, Allport thought it foolish to ignore any of the established theories of prejudice. But he also felt that some approaches were more relevant than others. In particular, he was of the opinion that cognitive factors and personality theories were better at explaining the causes of prejudice than a psychodynamic approach.*

Allport was convinced that a better understanding of prejudice could lead to an improvement in intergroup relations. But what was also highly important and central to Allport's theory of prejudice was his belief that prejudiced thinking was *the* cause of strained intergroup relations. Allport felt that if social scientists explained the *causes* of prejudice to policy-makers, then those policy-makers would take action and introduce laws designed to lessen prejudice and discrimination.

Allport's clear call for lawmakers to take action on the matter of prejudice was a very unusual position for a psychologist to take. To explain his stance, Allport said, "Law is intended only to control the outward expression of intolerance. But outward action, psychology knows, has an eventual effect upon inner habits of thought and feeling."[2]

Contribution In Context

When writing *The Nature of Prejudice,* Allport drew on all the existing academic literature studies. He looked not just at what had already been written on prejudice, but also at additional studies into other aspects of personality, such as the work by social psychologist Muzafer Sherif* on conformity.* Allport then used arguments from these different branches of personality psychology and social psychology to help him build his argument about prejudice. Such a method— looking to many different disciplines for answers—was new at the time. The existing approaches that Allport looked at included:

- historical
- psychodynamic
- personality
- religious
- cognitive
- developmental
- evolutionary
- sociocultural.

He devoted at least one chapter to examining prejudice through the lens of each of these approaches. But Allport expressed his view that cognitive factors were of the most relevance when it came to explaining how prejudices actually formed. Indeed, he came to rely on the work of cognitive psychologists when looking at prejudice formation.

Allport adapted ideas from what was then recent work in the cognitive sciences by Jerome Bruner* and George Zipf.* Bruner was a former student of Allport's who, by the 1950s, was himself an influential cognitive psychologist and linguist. It was from Zipf that Allport borrowed the least–effort principle to apply to stereotyping. In describing human behavior, Zipf wrote, "Each individual will adopt a course of action that will involve the expenditure of the probable least average of his work (by definition, least effort)."[3] Allport believed that human beings have limited cognitive resources with which to memorize, assess, and judge other people, so they inevitably turn to shortcuts. These shortcuts are often used to categorize people based on race or ethnicity, because these are clearly visible physical features. The recognizable characteristics then become used as markers of incorrect stereotypes, because people associate attributes to entire groups when they have no basis in reality. The adoption of the least–effort principle in relation to prejudice is fundamental to *The Nature of Prejudice* as a work, and making use of this principle in such a way was entirely original to Allport.

NOTES

1   Gordon W. Allport, *The Nature of Prejudice* (New York: Basic Books, 1979), XII.

2   Allport, *The Nature of Prejudice*, 442.

3   George Zipf, *Human Behavior and the Principle of Least Effort: An Introduction to Human Ecology* (Cambridge, MA: Addison-Wesley, 1949), 18.

SECTION 2
IDEAS

MAIN IDEAS

KEY POINTS

- Several factors—some of which are psychological—influence prejudice.

- Of these psychological factors, cognitive* factors—including the "least-effort principle,"* in which individuals use stereotypes as a shortcut to making a judgment—are particularly influential in developing prejudice. Allport also felt that because prejudice was caused by cognitive processes, anybody could develop prejudice.

- Allport knew that prejudiced people were the *least* likely to read *The Nature of Prejudice*. He felt that social scientists and policy-makers were responsible for creating improved intergroup relations and so tailored some of the text specifically to them.

Key Themes

Throughout *The Nature of Prejudice*, Gordon Allport emphasized that the development of prejudice and the discrimination that came about because of it were the result of many factors. In examining the causes of prejudice, he drew on several fields both inside and outside of psychology. These included:

- economics
- evolution theory
- history
- psychodynamic theory*
- cognitive theory
- personality psychology.*

> ❝ Why do human beings slip so easily into ethnic prejudice*? They do so because the two essential ingredients that we have discussed—*erroneous generalization* and *hostility*—are natural and common capacities of the human mind. ❞
>
> Gordon W. Allport, *The Nature of Prejudice*

Writing about these different disciplines, Allport said, "Each has something to teach us … None possesses a monopoly of insight, nor is any one safe as a solitary guide."[1] He did, however, believe that cognitive factors gave the best overall explanation for the foundation of prejudice, and so gave these cognitive factors the most attention throughout the text.

It was Allport's firm belief that if the many causes and subtleties of prejudice were better understood, this would lay the ground for him to introduce his big aim of using social action and well-informed public policy to minimize discrimination. In *The Nature of Prejudice*, he states, "We are now in a fair position to predict the consequences of segregation and of its abandonment; we know a good deal about the reaction of minority groups who are victimized by discrimination; we understand the impulsive protests against civil rights laws and the reasons why these are generally short-lived. These, and many other findings, represent potential contributions of social science to the clarification and improvement of legal ruling."[2]

Exploring The Ideas

Allport's core idea is the least-effort principle. He wrote, "Life is just too short to have differentiated concepts about everything. A few pathways are enough for us to walk in."[3] People's abilities to memorize and judge are limited, he noted, so they use mental shortcuts. The shortcuts used to categorize people are often based on broad visible features such as race and ethnicity. However, these are often overgeneralized, flawed stereotypes,* which lead people to think inaccurately that entire groups share certain characteristics.

Allport's least-effort principle is absolutely key to his analysis, because it normalizes prejudice as being the result of basic mental processes. This idea underpins his theory that prejudice is therefore a cognitive error and so supports his view that *all* human beings are susceptible to prejudice. Allport adapted the least-effort principle from the work of others in the field, such as the cognitive psychologist and linguist George Zipf.*[4] But when it was related to the idea of prejudice, the idea was entirely original to him.

The second core idea in *The Nature of Prejudice* is Allport's belief that if the *reasons* for prejudice were understood, this would then lead to action being taken that would decrease general prejudice. This in turn would lead to people behaving in less discriminatory ways. Allport assumed that once they were better informed about how and why prejudice happens, then social scientists, intellectuals, and politicians would all want to act to improve intergroup and interracial relations. He did anticipate, however, that policy-makers might resist making changes to the status quo because they would fear a backlash from the more prejudiced sections of the population. Allport provided lots of anecdotal evidence (that is, evidence based on unsubstantiated reports) *and* research findings to back up his view that this backlash wouldn't actually happen—even if laws were introduced to reduce discrimination.

Allport believed that any protest against potential anti-discrimination measures would fade away once the actual change had happened. As evidence for this, he cited the lack of resistance to the Fair Employment Practices Commission* Acts, which had been put in place to increase the job prospects of American minorities. Allport summarized his belief as follows: "Over and over again, it has been predicted that if discrimination is stopped dire consequences will follow—perhaps strikes or riots. Very seldom do they follow. What happens is that the verbal protest is greater than the demand for actual discrimination."[5]

Language And Expression

Allport's core ideas are communicated very clearly in *The Nature of Prejudice*. He drew on many different theories from a number of disciplines and backed up each particular theory's influence on the development of prejudice with hard data. Because his ultimate goal was to reduce prejudice, Allport wanted his book to be read by three broad audiences:

- American citizens (particularly white Protestant* males, because they were the largest group with the power to change attitudes)
- social scientists, because they would be able to improve our understanding of prejudice through science
- politicians/lawmakers everywhere, because they would be able to make laws to introduce real change.

Because he believed each of those groups needed to receive different messages, he wrote passages tailored specifically to each of them throughout the text.

Allport provided evidence to American citizens that prejudice was more widespread than most people in majority groups realized. He suggested to social scientists that they should focus on cognitive and personality factors as a basis to understanding prejudice. This was because he wanted to redirect the focus of future research into the subject. He also encouraged social scientists to do more applied research (that is, work of a more practical nature). Rather than producing studies that tried to uncover the *reasons* behind prejudice, Allport wanted them to undertake studies aimed at *reducing* discrimination. Finally, he hoped that once they understood *why* prejudice existed, politicians and lawmakers would use their powers to make laws that would help reduce it.

Allport was optimistic that change could be made for the better, and often mentioned his belief that public attitudes toward American minority groups and segregation were, in fact, already changing in the 1950s.

NOTES

1   Gordon W. Allport, *The Nature of Prejudice* (New York: Basic Books, 1979), 212.

2   Allport, *The Nature of Prejudice*, 441.

3   Allport, *The Nature of Prejudice*, 169.

4   George Zipf, *Human Behavior and the Principle of Least Effort: An Introduction to Human Ecology* (Cambridge, MA: Addison-Wesley, 1949), 18.

5   Allport, *The Nature of Prejudice*, 55.

MODULE 6
SECONDARY IDEAS

KEY POINTS

- Some prejudice* is the result of people conforming to what society thinks is normal.
- Intergroup contact,* in which there is increased contact with a different group, is a promising way to improve intergroup relations and may decrease prejudice.
- Allport was interested in examining how an interest in religion might affect a person's prejudice.

Other Ideas

The main focus of *The Nature of Prejudice* is on the influence that cognitive and personality factors have on the formation of prejudice. However, Gordon Allport also examined more specific factors, such as intergroup contact, conformity,* and religion. He looks at how each of these different elements affects prejudice and stereotyping. Put simply, intergroup contact considers how much contact a person has with members of other groups. By conformity, Allport refers to the extent that prejudice is a result of social norms. For example, if a person's peers all dislike a certain group of people, then that person is likely to conform to the peer group view.

The case of religion is complicated. Allport argued that religions typically promote tolerance and love, which might lower prejudice among their followers. However, religions are also ethnocentric,* meaning that most followers share a common identity and avoid those who do not share this identity. Allport described religion's role in prejudice as "paradoxical. It makes prejudice, and it unmakes prejudice."[1]

> ❝ It has sometimes been held that merely by assembling people without regard for race, color, religion, or national origin, we can thereby destroy stereotypes* and develop friendly attitudes. The case is not so simple. ❞
>
> Gordon Allport, *The Nature of Prejudice*

For Allport, cognition* and personality are broad factors—psychological processes that apply to everyone. But he does not consider intergroup contact, conformity, or religion to be general psychological processes that affect everyone. So while they are still important, these ideas are less central to his theory of the causes of prejudice. Allport noted, for example, that intergroup contact could not overtake other broad factors: "It would seem fair to conclude that contact, as a situational variable, cannot always overcome the personal variable in prejudice. This is true whenever the inner strain within the person is too tense, too insistent, to permit him to profit from the structure of the outer situation."[2]

Exploring The Ideas

Allport adapted his intergroup contact theory from previous studies showing that the more experience individuals have of other groups (be they racial, ethnic, religious, or something else), the better their attitudes toward those groups will be. But Allport suggested that the original understanding of intergroup contact theory was not enough. He added conditions, saying these particular conditions would make it easier for there to be a positive intergroup contact effect. He explained, "Prejudice (unless deeply rooted in the character structure of the individual) may be reduced by equal status contact between majority and minority groups in the pursuit of common goals. The effect is greatly enhanced if this contact is sanctioned by institutional supports (i.e. by law, custom, or local atmosphere), and if it is of a sort that leads to the perception of common interests and common humanity between members of two groups."[3] That formulation became known as "Allport's Intergroup Contact Theory."

In *The Nature of Prejudice*, Allport also emphasized that conformity played a significant role in forming prejudice. He believed that a certain amount of prejudice was due to people conforming to the views of their family, their peers, or society. As evidence of this, he quoted data from the US Air Force showing that most white recruits supported racial segregation of the Armed Forces. However, only half that number had a personal objection to being in a desegregated unit. Allport highlighted this finding among others as a reason why he was hopeful the levels of prejudice in society could be changed. He also highlighted this information as a reason why the government should clarify its stance on prejudice and discrimination.

For Allport, a lack of intergroup contact and a tendency to conform would most likely point to increased prejudice occurring. But he did not suggest that these factors could explain prejudice as extensively as broader cognitive and personality factors could.

Overlooked

The relationship between religion and prejudice may have received less attention than Allport would have wanted. Allport was a religious man himself, and had studied the links between religion and personality. After thoroughly examining the evidence, Allport found that people who are drawn to religious *institutions* to satisfy their own personal needs (what would later be called an "extrinsic orientation of religion") often showed more prejudice than average. These needs might be for security, status, comfort, or social support. However, Allport also found that people who learn and take on board the important beliefs of a religion (what would later be called an "intrinsic orientation of religion") were often lower in prejudice than average.

Today, theorists argue as to whether Allport's ideas here can really predict prejudice. Yet some researchers do find that similar ideas of what motivates religious people have a bearing on prejudice.[4]

Religion is the only area of prejudice research that Allport continued to look at after writing *The Nature of Prejudice*. So it would be reasonable to speculate that he would have been disappointed that less attention was paid to it.[5]

It is not clear why religion barely figures in modern discussions of *The Nature of Prejudice*. Perhaps it is something to do with the fact that this particular field of study in general tends not to focus on religion. Allport may have been referring to this when he wrote, "Many democratic personalities, to be sure, are not religious ... religion, however, is a large factor in most people's philosophy of life."[6]

NOTES

1   Gordon W. Allport, *The Nature of Prejudice* (New York: Basic Books, 1979), 413.

2   Allport, *The Nature of Prejudice*, 267.

3   Allport, *The Nature of Prejudice*, 267.

4   Gregory M. Herek, "Religious Orientation and Prejudice: A Comparison of Racial and Sexual Attitudes," *Personality and Social Psychology Bulletin* 13, no. 1 (1987): 34–44.

5   Gordon W. Allport and J. Michael Ross. "Personal Religious Orientation and Prejudice," *Journal of Personality and Social Psychology* 5, no. 4 (1967): 432.

6   Allport, *The Nature of Prejudice*, 425.

ACHIEVEMENT

KEY POINTS

- *The Nature of Prejudice* linked and organized the relevant research of the time and shaped future research on prejudice.*
- The book managed to reach a much wider audience than the world of academia alone.
- The text overlooked sexism as a huge example of everyday prejudice.

Assessing The Argument

In *The Nature of Prejudice*, Gordon Allport successfully examined and brought in all of the relevant research that existed to create a comprehensive work on the study of prejudice. The American social psychologist Thomas Pettigrew's statement makes this clear: "[The book's] table of contents … has in fact organized the scholarly study of the important concept of prejudice. *The Nature of Prejudice* delineated the area of study, set up its basic categories and problems, and cast it in a broad, eclectic framework that remains today."[1]

Pettigrew also wrote, "[Allport] once told me that [the book] was his proudest achievement because he thought it 'had done some good in the world.' He took particular pride in seeing it on sale in airports and drugstores. Indeed, [the paperback edition] became one of the best-selling social psychological books in publishing history."[2] These facts tend to confirm that Allport achieved his goal of reaching a broader, non-academic audience.

> ❝ This influential volume again brought together
> Gordon's two sides, science and social action. ❞
>
> Thomas F. Pettigrew,* "Gordon Willard Allport: A Tribute,"
> *Journal of Social Issues* 55, no. 3

Achievement In Context

Social psychology* and intergroup* relations researchers needed a
work to bring together and organize all the research that already
existed. Given how well Allport did that, it is no surprise that *The
Nature of Prejudice* successfully reached the academic community.
Allport thought, though, that reaching a non-academic audience
would be much more difficult. He believed it would be particularly
hard to spread his message to individuals who denied the widespread
existence of prejudice, and to people who thought there was nothing
wrong with being biased against other groups.

He wrote, "Anyone who works in the field of intercultural
relations knows how often in his community he hears the remark,
'There is no problem.' Parents, teachers, public officials, police,
community leaders seem unaware of the undercurrents of friction and
hostility. Until or unless violence breaks out, 'There is no problem.'"[3]
Allport admitted that prejudiced people were the least likely to read
the text. And, even if they did, they would probably criticize it.

Allport's solution was to make suggestions to politicians and
lawmakers within the pages of the book itself. *The Nature of Prejudice*
supplied hard evidence to back up all of its ideas and arguments.
Allport agreed that prejudiced individuals might protest against any
attempts by the government to promote racial integration. But he
believed that they were unlikely to *act* once such policies had actually
been passed as law. In the years following the publication of *The Nature
of Prejudice*, US legislators and courts did, in fact, enact and uphold
several laws intended to desegregate* public facilities and provide

increased civil rights. To an extent, the passing of those acts can be seen to support Allport's optimistic view that policy-makers could indeed bring in legislation that would improve intergroup relations in the United States.

Limitations

There are not many aspects of *The Nature of Prejudice* that have failed the test of time or been proved wrong. Some of the groups Allport focused on—African Americans, Latinos, and immigrants—are still among the minority groups that are the most discriminated against in the United States today. But the text was intended to be all-encompassing. It was not designed to describe prejudice and discrimination among some groups, but not others. While prejudice against some of the groups mentioned by Allport is less relevant today (anti-communism is a good example, because communism—which eliminates private ownership—is no longer a major political system), prejudice against other groups (homophobia* and Islamophobia,* for example) is more relevant. Allport pointed out that visible characteristics such as race and ethnicity are often used as markers of difference and therefore prejudice. But he rightly also said that other less visible markers such as religion and ideology can also cause prejudice by the same processes.

Allport argued that prejudice exists across cultures and across history. But despite this, he devoted only a few paragraphs to prejudice and discrimination against women. This suggests that sexism was not particularly obvious to American psychologists in the 1940s and early 1950s. In the collection of essays published in tribute to *The Nature of Prejudice*, John Dovidio* wrote, "Perhaps a victim of his time, [Allport] overlooked, as [Laurie] Rudman* describes it, the 'ordinariness of gender prejudice.'" Allport argued for the presence and universality of prejudice. But he neglected the largest group of human beings facing widespread prejudice and discrimination: women.

NOTES

1   Thomas Pettigrew, preface to *The Nature of Prejudice* (New York: Basic Books, 1979), xiii.

2   Thomas F. Pettigrew, "Gordon Willard Allport: A Tribute," *Journal of Social Issues* 55, no. 3 (1999): 420.

3   Gordon W. Allport, *The Nature of Prejudice* (New York: Basic Books, 1979), 464.

PLACE IN THE AUTHOR'S WORK

KEY POINTS

- Allport used interdisciplinary approaches to answer psychological questions about personality, with the hope of bringing about social good.

- He wrote *The Nature of Prejudice* toward the end of his academic life, intending to explore many different theories of why prejudice occurs. His work established the interdisciplinary approach in the field of social psychology.

- *The Nature of Prejudice* is his most famous work, but Allport wrote other seminal (key) works in the field of personality, including *Personality: A Psychological Interpretation* and *Pattern and Growth in Personality*.

Positioning

The Nature of Prejudice was Gordon Allport's fourth book. It was published in 1954 during the later stages of his academic career at Harvard University and is the most famous of his works. It is considered a seminal text in social psychology, having strongly influenced later developments in the field. But Allport is regarded above all as a personality psychologist.* His early career was dominated by his works on personality psychology, such as *Personality: A Psychological Interpretation*. He continued to publish on this topic throughout his career, including his last major work, *Pattern and Growth in Personality*.

Allport also published a number of articles on prejudice throughout his career. Most were written at around the same time as *The Nature of Prejudice*. Afterward, however, he wrote just a few prejudice theory papers, on the role of religion and prejudice.[1]

> ❝ Scholars have generally neglected the moral continuity between Allport's work on personality and the 'character' ideal of social ethics.* ❞
>
> Professor Ian Nicholson, *Inventing Personality: Gordon Allport and the Science of Selfhood*

Integration

Allport examined many topics during his career, spanning several subdisciplines of psychology, including personality and social* and cognitive* psychology. He was primarily a personality psychologist and is known as one of the founders of the field. Indeed, he published several important and influential works on personality.[2] But while these texts address different questions, all of his works have a common theme: to explain what personality is. Allport tried to achieve a balance between methods and theories, and often gave more consideration to rival theories than other academics might have done. The American social psychologist Thomas Pettigrew* wrote, "Gordon sought an eclectic balance for both methods and theory. His two famous volumes on personality—*Personality: A Psychological Interpretation* and *Pattern and Growth in Personality*—illustrate this dominant feature of his work. He urged, for example, the use of both ideographic (individual) and nomothetic (universal) methods because he thought the discipline relied too heavily on nomothetic approaches." Pettigrew continued, "This was an expansionist,* not an exclusionist,* view. He simply sought a reasonable trade-off between accuracy and adequacy. He thought the two approaches together would make for 'a broadened psychology.'"[3]

Allport hoped many of his works would bring about social change. He believed that social scientists could and should use their work to inform policy decisions. In *The Nature of Prejudice* he suggested that perhaps the timing was right for social scientists to help with social legislation. He wrote, "The question now arises whether modern social science can be of practical assistance to courts and to legislatures, so that erroneous assumptions concerning the psychological and social consequences of a proposed action might be guarded against. In the nineteenth century, this question would have been premature; in the twentieth century perhaps it is not."[4]

Significance

Despite Allport being primarily seen as the founder of personality psychology, *The Nature of Prejudice* is still his most famous and most frequently quoted work. His two personality psychology texts cited most often—*Personality: A Psychological Interpretation* and *Pattern and Growth in Personality*[5]—are seminal works that established the field. In these personality texts, Allport develops his "trait* approach" to personality psychology. A trait is a lasting and steady characteristic in someone's personality that makes him or her behave in certain ways. It could be a description such as "outgoing," "intelligent," or "kind." In 1936, Allport went through a dictionary picking out more than 4,000 words that can be used to describe such characteristics. But he believed that we need only a small handful of these to really define who we are, and that they can be arranged in three levels: central traits, cardinal traits, and secondary traits. Central traits are the few traits that best describe us. A cardinal trait is one central trait that could emerge to become a person's defining personality trait. Secondary traits are those that tend to emerge in certain circumstances. For example, when someone always gets impatient or anxious when asked to wait in line.

The Nature of Prejudice is the most important work on the study of prejudice, which is still considered an important research topic in the discipline of social psychology today. Personality is itself a major part of the discipline of psychology, and Allport's two best-known works on this subject both established and shaped the discipline. Indeed, all three of his best-known books are seminal works, but the topics they discuss have different scopes. The study of prejudice has a greater reach than personality psychology, because personality psychology focuses on the personal. Therefore, it could not have the same social consequences that Allport hoped to produce through his theory of prejudice.

NOTES

1   Gordon W. Allport and J. Michael Ross, "Personal Religious Orientation and Prejudice," *Journal of Personality and Social Psychology* 5, no. 4 (1967): 432.

2   Gordon W. Allport, *Personality: A Psychological Interpretation* (New York: Henry Holt, 1937).

3   Thomas F. Pettigrew, "Gordon Willard Allport: A Tribute," *Journal of Social Issues* 55, no. 3 (1999): 418–9.

4   Gordon W. Allport, *The Nature of Prejudice* (New York: Basic Books, 1979), 441.

5   Gordon W. Allport, *Pattern and Growth in Personality* (New York: Harcourt, 1961).

SECTION 3
IMPACT

MODULE 9
THE FIRST RESPONSES

KEY POINTS

- Allport was criticized for his assumption that prejudice and stereotyping* were important reasons why discrimination exists, and for his definition of prejudice as being exclusively caused by feelings of hatred.

- Allport did not directly respond to these criticisms. But his defenders argue that prejudice is one of many important causes of discrimination. In addition, his limited definition of prejudice is considered equal to that of other researchers of his time.

- These criticisms are relatively minor compared with the many ideas from the text that continue to dominate the field.

Criticism

There was no widespread academic debate or movement that criticized Gordon Allport's *The Nature of Prejudice* in the years immediately following its publication in 1954. However, decades later, in the 1980s, a handful of social scientists—including the psychologist Irwin Katz—began to contest Allport's assumption that there were direct links that led from prejudice to discrimination. Katz claimed that these links between prejudice and discrimination were weak. He believed that prejudice was not, in fact, the main cause of discrimination, and that other contributing factors should receive more attention. The factors Katz thought should be considered were:

> ❝ Forty years of social psychological research have not provided strong support for Allport's assumption that prejudice* causes discrimination nor an explanation of the substantial long-term movement in the majority's racial sentiments and beliefs. ❞
>
> Professor Irwin Katz,* social and political psychologist

- actual group differences
- conformity*
- appeasement (for example, businesses not hiring African Americans for fear that it would affect business relations with white Americans)
- historical institutional inequalities.[1]

Katz also argued that these institutional-level inequalities (such as segregated housing) are difficult to change, and that this form of discrimination is not the result of any one individual's prejudice or malicious attitude.

Allport is known for developing the cognitive* approach to the study of prejudice, but Katz believed that the cognitive approach went on to become overused. He wrote that "[Allport's] perspective fosters an overemphasis on laboratory studies of internal psychological functions to the neglect of overt actions as they unfold in naturalistic multi-ethnic settings. It tends to overlook the societal context of intergroup phenomena."[2]

In addition, Katz, Peter Glick,* Susan Fiske,* and others argued that the idea of prejudice as understood by Allport was limited. Allport defined prejudice as "an antipathy* based on faulty and inflexible generalization."[3] Later research, however, showed that there is prejudice without antipathy, such as paternalistic* beliefs. This is when the group in power thinks that they need to make decisions for some other groups because those groups will function better that way. Paternalism and other forms of prejudice without antipathy were shown to have effects just as bad as those caused by prejudice resulting from hatred.

Researchers who later said that Allport's definition of prejudice was too limited did not blame him for that oversight. Glick and his co-authors noted that, when overlooking paternalism, Allport had perhaps been "a victim of his time." Glick wrote, "Prejudice comes in qualitatively different forms, such as an ostensibly benevolent paternalism that disadvantages groups without apparent antipathy, that Allport and, for many years, the rest of the field, simply missed."[4]

Responses

Allport, it seems, did not address those criticisms. He lived for only 13 years after the publication of *The Nature of Prejudice*, and nearly all the works he wrote afterward were either contributions to his trait* and personality theories or short autobiographical essays. Overall, there was not much criticism of the ideas in *The Nature of Prejudice*, and many of the psychologists who did argue with any of Allport's points presented their disagreement with him as minor. Even Fiske, who criticized the narrow definition of prejudice used by Allport, defended the writer's idea that prejudice was a primary cause of discrimination. She explained that the low-level links between prejudice and discrimination—which Katz had used to argue that the theory was wrong—were in fact typical of links found between attitudes and behavior in other areas of psychology.[5]

Conflict And Consensus

Neither Allport nor his supporters gave a public response to the few critics of the original text. However, these criticisms did eventually lead to fruitful research decades later—long after Allport's death. A number of researchers in the 1980s and 1990s (including Katz, Glick, and Fiske) supported the idea that prejudice does not necessarily arise out of hatred toward another group, which was the way Allport had defined it. In particular, research on benevolent sexism and racism* supported the idea that thoughts and behaviors that at first seem to protect disadvantaged groups are statistically proven to be linked with malevolent (i.e. hostile) forms of prejudice and discrimination. When studying benevolent sexism, researchers found that people who agreed with what on the surface looked like harmless or kindly attitudes (such as the belief that women must be protected by men) are also more likely to agree with malevolent attitudes toward and to discriminate against women in a number of different ways.

It is worth saying that, at the time Allport wrote the text, malevolent forms of prejudice were so common that they perhaps obscured the existence of benign instances. Psychologist Laurie Rudman* described the pre-civil rights context and its influence on Allport's limited definition of sexism: "How did Allport miss the ordinariness of gender prejudice? Historically and cross-culturally, women have traditionally been subordinate to men, creating a situation for Allport like that of the proverbial fish, blind to the water he swims in. Further, women themselves appeared to be content with the water, so Allport was not ignoring their complaints."[6] As the American Civil Rights Movement* progressed, obvious discrimination and malevolent prejudice slowly lessened. In its wake, benevolent forms of prejudice became more apparent. It is possible therefore to suggest that if Allport had written the text a couple of decades later, he would have considered benevolent forms of prejudice.

NOTES

1   Irwin Katz, "Gordon Allport's *The Nature of Prejudice*," *Political Psychology* 12, no. 1 (1991): 125–57.

2   Katz, "Gordon Allport's *The Nature of Prejudice*," 152.

3   Gordon W. Allport, *The Nature of Prejudice* (New York: Basic Books, 1979), 10.

4   John F. Dovidio et al., *On the Nature of Prejudice: Fifty Years after Allport* (New York: Wiley, 2005), 11.

5   Susan T. Fiske, "On the Road: Comment on the Cognitive Stereotyping Literature in Pettigrew and Martin," *Journal of Social Issues* 43, no. 1 (1987): 113–18.

6   Laurie A. Rudman, "Rejection of Women? Beyond Prejudice as Antipathy," in Dovidio et al., *On the Nature of Prejudice*, 107.

THE EVOLVING DEBATE

KEY POINTS

- Allport and *The Nature of Prejudice* brought about a cognitive* approach to studying prejudice.*

- This approach offered solid evidence to prove the idea that prejudice and stereotyping are largely a result of the normal processing of social information.

- Allport's followers continue to prove the value of many of his ideas, such as his intergroup contact hypothesis.*

Uses And Problems

The Nature of Prejudice was one of the first works to recognize the importance of cognition in the study of intergroup relations. Because of this, the text fueled a broader debate between cognitive approaches (which focused on internal attitudes, motivations, and beliefs) and behaviorism,* which largely ignored cognitive processes. Allport also successfully shifted the focus of prejudice researchers away from psychodynamic* factors and toward universal cognitive factors. In those two particular ways, the text reset the path of prejudice research for decades.

The cognitive revolution* gained followers in the 1950s and eventually replaced behaviorism as the leading framework for study in the cognitive sciences. Allport died in 1967, but nonetheless the field of social cognition* was born in the late 1960s. This was the most important result of the cognitive revolution in social psychology. Social cognition became the dominant framework for studying prejudice in the 1970s and much of its influence continued all the way through to the twenty-first century. Henri Tajfel,* a psychologist and

> " Insofar as Gordon Allport influenced the agenda of modern social psychological* research on intergroup relations, it was probably in the direction of making negative group attitudes and stereotypes* the central topic of inquiry, and the cognitive perspective (whereby ethnic categorization and stereotyping are viewed as an instance of ordinary information processing) the dominant theoretical approach. "
>
> Professor Irwin Katz,* social and political psychologist

leading researcher on intergroup relations after Allport, wrote, "As the late Gordon Allport ... and many others pointed out, stereotypes arise from a process of categorization. They introduce simplicity and order where there is complexity and nearly random variation."[1]

As the social cognition approach to studying prejudice moved forward, researchers applied the use of *schemas*—set patterns of thought or behavior that help organize associated ideas, objects, groups, and so on. Alongside other social cognition researchers, Susan Fiske* put forward the idea that when schemas become "activated," they bring to mind other information linked to the original concept.

Patricia Devine* later applied that particular framework to establish the current notion of stereotypes, which adds subtleties to Allport's original concept.[2] Quoting Allport, Devine wrote, "Many classic and contemporary theorists have suggested that prejudice is an inevitable consequence of ordinary categorization (stereotyping) processes. The basic argument of the 'inevitability of prejudice' perspective is that as long as stereotypes exist, prejudice will follow ... The inevitability of prejudice approach, however, overlooks an important distinction between knowledge of a cultural stereotype and acceptance or endorsement of the stereotype." Devine argued that if a given stereotype is not accepted as valid by a person, it will not necessarily lead to the negative consequences of prejudice detailed by Allport in *The Nature of Prejudice*—not even if the person is aware of the stereotype and has, in fact, activated it in his or her mind.

Schools Of Thought

Today, a cognitive perspective is the most frequently used framework in which to study prejudice. Many prejudice researchers examine unconscious, or automatic, cognitions related to prejudice and stereotyping.[3] Allport, though, most often characterized references to prejudice and stereotyping as conscious processes. Later, social cognition researchers did begin to investigate how much the stereotype formation process happens on an unconscious level. Much of the research after Allport brought together his work on prejudice with more recent studies by cognitive psychologists on unconscious processes. These include priming* and implicit memory.* Priming describes the influence that stimuli from outside our conscious awareness can have on our behavior, emotions, and cognition. Social psychologists then moved on to work on the effect that implicit memory has on prejudice and stereotypes. They began to develop work on "implicit bias,"* which refers to group preferences, prejudices, or stereotypes that are outside of conscious awareness.

Advances in cognitive psychology directly influenced research on implicit bias, but this was in line with the path set out in *The Nature of Prejudice*. Such research took several assumptions that had their roots in Allport's work and developed them further. These assumptions include Allport's idea that the use of stereotypes makes judgment and categorization of objects and people easier, and will therefore influence behavior.

A dramatic example of this implicit bias is "shooter bias."* This happens as the result of stereotypic associations between one group of people and violence or weapons, leading other people to misperceive members of that group as a threat or as holding a weapon when in fact they are not. Psychologist Joshua Correll,* who first examined the effect, stated, "In the United States, [dangerous] stereotypes are frequently applied to black people—particularly to black men … Using [a video game] task, we find robust evidence of bias, such that participants shoot an armed target more quickly and more frequently when that target is black (rather than white), but they decide not to shoot an unarmed target more quickly and more frequently when the target is white (rather than black). In essence, participants are faster and more accurate when targets conform to the cultural stereotype that blacks are dangerous."[4]

In Current Scholarship

The most fruitful idea in the text—Allport's intergroup contact hypothesis—directly inspired hundreds of studies in the decades after the book's publication. A former student of Allport's, Thomas Pettigrew,* was one of the lead investigators examining how true Allport's hypothesis actually was. He summarized it as saying that "contact between groups under optimal conditions could effectively reduce intergroup prejudice. In particular, Allport held that reduced prejudice will result when four features of the contact situation are present: equal status between the groups in the situation; common goals; intergroup cooperation; and the support of authorities, law, or custom."

Pettigrew argued that Allport's work is still deeply relevant to current scholarship. He co-authored a review of the literature in this area (a meta-analysis*) in 2006. Here he examined hundreds of studies that looked at Allport's contact hypothesis, including the influence of the four features Allport considered essential. Pettigrew concluded, "Allport's conditions should not be regarded as necessary for producing positive contact outcomes, as researchers have often assumed in the past. Rather, they act as facilitating conditions that enhance the tendency for positive contact outcomes to emerge."[5]

However, scholars had already anticipated this result before Pettigrew proved it in 2006. The US Supreme Court cited Allport in a discrimination case against people with learning difficulties, noting, "Most important, lengthy and continuing isolation of the retarded has perpetuated the ignorance, irrational fears, and stereotyping that long have plagued them."[6]

NOTES

1   H. Tajfel, *Human Groups and Social Categories* (Cambridge: Cambridge University Press, 1981), 132.

2   Patricia G. Devine, "Stereotypes and Prejudice: Their Automatic and Controlled Components," *Journal of Personality and Social Psychology* 56, no. 1 (1989): 5–18.

3   Devine, "Stereotypes and Prejudice," 5–18.

4   J. Correll et al., "Event-Related Potentials and the Decision to Shoot: The Role of Threat Perception and Cognitive Control," *Journal of Experimental Social Psychology* 42 (2006): 120–8.

5   Thomas F. Pettigrew and Linda R. Tropp, "A Meta-analytic Test of Intergroup Contact Theory," *Journal of Personality and Social Psychology* 90, no. 5 (2006): 751–83.

6   Cleburne v. Cleburne Living Center, Inc., 473 US 432—Supreme Court 1985, 464.

MODULE 11
IMPACT AND INFLUENCE TODAY

KEY POINTS

- *The Nature of Prejudice* is regarded as the foundational work in the psychological study of prejudice.*

- Programs to improve intergroup relations based on Allport's ideas—such as diversity training* in the business environment—have not proved to be completely successful as yet.

- New research seems to suggest that the ways in which diversity programs are run may be as important as the actual techniques used.

Position

The Nature of Prejudice remains relevant today, particularly to academics and social scientists. In 2005, a collection of essays was published, updating the status of Gordon Allport's core themes. Many of the most influential prejudice researchers in psychology, such as John Dovidio and Susan Fiske,* contributed to *On the Nature of Prejudice: Fifty Years after Allport,*[1] and each of them paid respect to Allport and his influence on the field. Dovidio and his co-editors wrote, "Half a century after its publication, *The Nature of Prejudice* remains the most widely cited work on prejudice. The scope and endurance of its influence has been nothing short of remarkable."

The book's editors said that one reason for the continuing influence of Allport's text was his wide-ranging treatment of the study of prejudice. He provided a number of theories and new ideas rather than just one notion, drawing from a range of disciplines as he did so. Dovidio and his co-editors added, "Allport embraced seemingly

> **"There is no debate that Gordon Allport's (1954/1979)** *The Nature of Prejudice* is the foundational work for the social psychology of prejudice.**"**
>
> John F. Dovidio,* Peter Glick,* and Laurie A. Rudman,* "Introduction: Reflecting on *The Nature of Prejudice*: Fifty Years after Allport," in *On the Nature of Prejudice: Fifty Years after Allport*

contradictory views at different points in *The Nature of Prejudice*. Thus, he has been many things to many thinkers. For example, Allport is the founder of the cognitive approach to prejudice, which views stereotyping* and categorization as normal and inevitable by-products of how people think. Yet he also viewed prejudice as a fundamentally irrational hatred, born of ignorance and the ego-defensive maneuvers of people with weak personality structures … From the standpoint of generating ideas, he could hardly have been more successful; his book has been, and will likely continue to be, mined productively by generations of theorists and researchers."

Interaction

Some prejudice researchers argue that programs intended to improve intergroup relations—many of which originated from Allport's text—are actually ineffective. Sociologist Frank Dobbin* and his co-authors summarize their findings about the ineffectiveness of diversity training for American managers in corporate settings: "On average, programs designed to reduce bias among managers responsible for hiring and promotion have not worked. Neither diversity training to extinguish stereotypes, nor diversity performance evaluations to provide feedback and oversight to people making hiring and promotion decisions, have accomplished much."[2] Nonetheless, research is still going on to try to maximize the effect of diversity training programs. And the authors believe it is possible that programs that can become effective will be developed. In this respect they show the same optimism as Allport himself in the battle to overcome prejudice.

The Continuing Debate

While study of the effectiveness of existing diversity programs continues, many researchers are now looking at new methods to reduce intergroup prejudice. Other psychologists examining and putting such programs into practice argue that, under certain conditions, these diversity programs *are* successful. In a review of the relevant studies, psychologists Walter G. Stephan* and Cookie White Stephan* found that a range of diversity programs were effective in reducing prejudice, as long as the programs were longer than three hours. However, the form that the program takes is also important. It seems that, in general, in-person programs (rather than online programs) that are run in ways that bring people closer together— such as role-playing—work better than lecture-based diversity programs. Stephan and Stephan summarize the state of current work on the effectiveness of these programs: "At the present state of our knowledge, it appears that the manner in which the [diversity] programs are conducted may be more important than the specific techniques that are employed."[3]

Assessing Allport's earlier work on diversity programs, Stephan and Stephan wrote, "Allport's focus on the evaluation of intergroup relations programs and his attention to evaluation design seem completely modern." They too added an optimistic note, saying, "We also think that Allport would be excited to see how the types of programs he identified in 1954 have flourished and become integrated into institutions such as schools and business organizations."[4]

NOTES

1   John F. Dovidio et al., *On the Nature of Prejudice: Fifty Years after Allport* (New York: Wiley, 2005).

2   F. Dobbin et al., "Diversity Management in Corporate America," *Contexts* 6 (2007): 26.

3   Walter G. Stephan and Cookie White Stephan, "Intergroup Relations Program Evaluation," in Dovidio et al., *On the Nature of Prejudice*, 439.

4   Stephan and Stephan, "Intergroup Relations Program Evaluation," 442.

WHERE NEXT?

KEY POINTS

- Allport's text will continue to serve as a reference for the origin of the modern psychological study of prejudice.*
- Its dominant themes—such as the role of cognition* and stereotypes*— are timeless and thus are still a major part of research on prejudice.
- Allport's book remains an essential text because it is so comprehensive in its study of how prejudice is formed.

Potential

Gordon Allport's *The Nature of Prejudice* is likely to persist as the key text on the psychology of prejudice. Although the forms and levels of prejudice change over time and between cultures, prejudice is persistent and culturally universal. So the work's main aim—to improve intergroup relations by shedding light on and reducing prejudice and stereotyping*—is timeless. The ideas, data, and theories presented in the text also remain relevant and are likely to stay that way. In particular, Allport's focus on the cognitive determinants* of prejudice and stereotyping is likely to persist as the most important framework for study in this area for some time to come.

It is difficult to see where there might be further development of the ideas contained in *The Nature of Prejudice*, largely because so much time and research has already been dedicated to it. However, it seems that some of the areas that Allport did not cover will continue to grow as subjects of research alongside the cognitive framework. In particular, the role played by emotions in prejudice and the effect of discrimination on people who are stigmatized (marked out as

> **❝** Contemporary prejudice researchers and scholars regularly refer back to this work not only for apt quotations, but also for inspiration. **❞**
>
> John F. Dovidio,* Peter Glick,* and Laurie A. Rudman,* "Introduction: Reflecting on *The Nature of Prejudice*: Fifty Years after Allport," in *On the Nature of Prejudice: Fifty Years after Allport*

undesirable or unusual)—such as people with disabilities—are both now major areas of research with more potential for growth.[1] Allport did briefly cover the effect of discrimination on stigmatized groups, and his thoughts have helped shape advances that have since been made in this area. The psychologists Eliot R. Smith* and Diane M. Mackie,* meanwhile, explained the increased attention paid to the study of the role of emotion in forming prejudices when they wrote "New theoretical ideas began to emerge, which considered a broader range of emotions—such as irritation, anxiety, guilt, and even positive emotions—and not only the anger and hatred that Allport had discussed."[2]

Future Directions

Gordon Allport wrote about the need for applied studies on prejudice in *The Nature of Prejudice*, and this seems set to continue as a fruitful area of research. Social psychologist Jennifer Eberhardt* has looked at several instances of bias at the society level. She has also examined the different influences that race can have on policing and court judgments. Following in the tradition of Allport, she looks at what effect stereotyping plays in this area. In describing her work, Eberhardt particularly notes the influence that stereotypes of African Americans have on attitudes toward juvenile prison sentencing: "We find that race can have a sweeping effect even when people consider the same crime. Prompting people to think of a single black (rather than white) juvenile offender leads them to express greater support for sentencing all juveniles to life without parole when they have committed serious violent crimes."[3]

Summary

The Nature of Prejudice remains a seminal work. It is required reading for any student of prejudice and is the text in which the influential intergroup contact theory* was first developed. In addition, Allport's ideas in the book were at the forefront of the cognitive revolution* and the birth of the field of social cognition*—two movements that went on to dominate social psychology into the twenty-first century. The text is also historically informative, providing evidence of some of the earliest uses of social cognition in social psychology, uses that arrived before the cognitive revolution. Both the original and the adopted ideas found in *The Nature of Prejudice* underpinned the understanding of prejudice within the American Civil Rights Movement.* Most social scientists in the 1950s and 1960s were supportive of the movement, and several participated in it to some degree. Some also helped drive through anti-discrimination and anti-segregation laws using evidence of prejudice found in Allport's book.

Beyond *The Nature of Prejudice*, Allport is known as one of the founders of personality psychology* and of trait* theories of personality. In a 2002 study that attempted to quantify the influence of twentieth-century psychologists, Allport was ranked 11th in the field.[4] What really makes *The Nature of Prejudice* important and what sets it apart from similar works, however, is its depth, balance, and accuracy. Allport gave detailed and fair consideration to many different theories of prejudice. This was hugely important, giving weight to his firm beliefs that prejudice has multiple causes—and that to ignore any of them would be very foolish.

NOTES

1   Jennifer Crocker and Brenda Major, "Social Stigma and Self-Esteem: The Self-Protective Properties of Stigma," *Psychological Review* 96, no. 4 (1989): 608–30.

2   Eliot R. Smith and Diane M. Mackie, "Aggression, Hatred, and Other Emotions," in John F. Dovidio et al., *On the Nature of Prejudice: Fifty Years after Allport* (New York: Wiley, 2005), 364.

3   Jennifer L. Eberhardt, "The Race Factor in Trying Juveniles as Adults," *New York Times*, June 5, 2012, accessed January 31, 2015, http://www.nytimes.com/roomfordebate/2012/06/05/when-to-punish-a-young-offender-and-when-to-rehabilitate/the-race-factor-in-trying-juveniles-as-adults.

4   Steven J. Haggbloom et al., "The 100 Most Eminent Psychologists of the 20th Century," *Review of General Psychology* 6, no. 2 (2002): 139–52.

GLOSSARY

GLOSSARY OF TERMS

American Civil Rights Movement: a social movement in the United States that aimed to outlaw discrimination and increase the social standing of disadvantaged minority groups. Much of the movement centered on the treatment of African Americans, although other repressed minorities (such as Jewish Americans) were also involved.

Antipathy: an aversion toward something or another person or group.

Authoritarian: expecting strict obedience as opposed to favoring personal freedom.

Behaviorism: see *Psychological Behaviorism*.

Benevolent sexism and racism: attitudes and evaluations that may appear positive, but are actually damaging to group equity. These attitudes are often condescending or patriarchal, and are frequently related to other forms of malevolent prejudice and discrimination.

Catharsis: the process in which intense or repressed emotions are released, providing the individual a sense of relief and renewal.

Clinical psychology: the branch of psychology that integrates science, theory, and clinical practice in order to diagnose and treat mental illness and disability

Cognition: the study of mental processes, including attention, memory, reasoning, and perception.

Cognitive determinants: factors that create outcomes or effects in behavior.

Cognitive revolution: a broad movement beginning in the 1950s in several fields, such as psychology, anthropology, and linguistics. This movement focused on studying the internal thoughts, attitudes, motivations, and values used by human beings to make sense of and interact with the world.

Conformity: a way of behaving that matches the standard of a group or society.

De Facto **(concerning fact) segregation/discrimination:** this was not mandated by law, but existed because of social conventions or voluntary reasons (such as people of different races choosing to live in different neighborhoods).

De Jure **(concerning law) segregation/discrimination:** this existed because of local laws—often known as "Jim Crow laws"—that mandated racial segregation and discrimination. In the United States, these were typically state and local laws establishing racial segregation that exceeded or contradicted federal laws banning inequitable treatment in public settings.

Developmental psychology: the branch of psychology that is concerned with the cognitive development of human beings over time, with a primary focus on the formative years of childhood.

Diversity training: a course of instruction designed to improve the cultural awareness and communication skills of those taking part, often in a business/work setting, in order to encourage inclusion of different identity groups and to prevent discrimination.

Ethnocentric: a way of looking at things from the perspective of your own culture, and the belief that this is better or more important than other cultures and perspectives.

Exclusionist: contrasted with an expansionist approach, describes a common tendency in psychology to study individuals and societies separately using different scientific approaches.

Expansionist: contrasted with an exclusionist approach, describes Allport's attempt to broaden the science of psychology by avoiding the tendency to treat the study of universal phenomena and individual phenomena separately. Represents a more holistic, interdisciplinary method of study.

Fair Employment Practices Commission: this was created by U.S. President Franklin D. Roosevelt★ to help African Americans and other minorities obtain jobs in home-front industries during World War II. The Commission ruled that companies with government contracts should not discriminate based on race or religion. However, the US Congress never approved those acts.

Genocide: the targeted destruction of a particular ethnic group.

Gestalt psychology: field of psychology, holistic in the sense that it proposes that perception is the product of complex interactions among various stimuli. In opposition to behaviorists, Gestalt psychologists believe that cognitive processes are organized and are the key to understanding psychology.

Holocaust: the mass murder of civilians and Jews in particular by the Nazis during World War II.

Homophobia: discrimination or prejudice against homosexuals.

Human relations movement: a collective term given to the efforts of private groups such as the Commission for Interracial Cooperation, which created educational programs in the period after World War II in an effort to "cure" the problem of prejudice. Such groups sponsored a number of field studies and social research projects, but avoided addressing the political and societal underpinnings of racial prejudice, such as racial segregation. Their work helped shape Allport's conception of contact theory.

Implicit bias: group preferences, prejudices, or stereotypes that are outside conscious awareness.

Implicit memory: a memory of which one has no conscious awareness.

IQ (Intelligence Quotient): a number that is intended to represent your intelligence in comparison with the average for your age. It is measured using standardized tests.

Intergroup contact hypothesis: Allport claimed that contact with members of other groups improves attitudes toward that group and diminishes prejudice overall, as long as a series of conditions are met, such as equal status between those in contact.

Islamophobia: discrimination or prejudice against followers of the Islamic faith.

Jim Crow (Laws): laws put in place by state and federal governments to stop blacks from attaining greater equality in the period in American history from the end of Reconstruction in 1877 until the civil rights movements of the 1950s and 1960s.

Least-effort principle: maintains that the primary aim of all human decision-making and problem-solving is to expend the least amount of effort in order to accomplish a given task. Also known as Zipf's law, after Harvard professor George Kingsley Zipf who proposed the principle in 1949.

Meta-analysis: data analysis using a range of different studies of the same core subject from a variety of sources. This is generally used to measure wider trends.

Multiple causation: the philosophical idea that most things that occur are likely to be the result not just one cause, but rather multiple causes. In psychology, it is an important notion for the scientific study of emotions and behavior, which are likely to be the result of multiple influencing factors.

Neurologist: specialist in treating diseases of the nervous system.

Paternalistic: behavior that restricts people's rights and responsibilities while claiming that it is for their own good.

Personality psychology: a field of psychology that studies variation between individuals in terms of their attributes, traits, performance, behavior, and so forth.

Prejudice: a bias against someone or something that is based on a preconceived idea rather than personal experience or knowledge.

Priming: a product of unconscious memory, in which exposure to one stimulus results in changes in the response to another.

Proactive: initiating an action or creating a situation rather than just reacting after something has already happened.

Protestant: a Christian Church that emerged during the Reformation. It denies the authority of the Pope and places emphasis on Biblical truth and a personalized faith.

Psychoanalysis: see *Psychodynamic/Freudian Psychodynamic Thinking.*

Psychodynamic/Freudian psychodynamic thinking: an approach to psychology emphasizing early childhood experiences as the dominant psychological forces underlying all human understanding and behavior. It is especially concerned with the relationship between conscious and unconscious motivation.

Psychological behaviorism: a major theory of learning that dominated psychology throughout the twentieth century, particularly in the middle of the century. The theory tended to view cognitive factors (thinking) as less relevant to behavior than other psychological theories.

Racial desegregation: putting and end to the practice of separating people according to race.

Repressed affect: characterized by inhibited emotions and desires which would otherwise cause an individual distress, and which are instead manifested as apathy or anxiety.

Self-alienation: The process of distancing oneself from one's own emotions, especially as a symptom of mental illness or emotional trauma.

Shooter bias: a tendency to both misperceive weapons and quickly recognize weapons when held by groups who are stereotypically associated with violence and weapons (such as African Americans in the United States).

Social cognition: using cognitive psychology approaches, methods, and theorizing human memory and information processing to study social phenomena. Some of the original social cognitive thinking is found in *The Nature of Prejudice*.

Social ethics: rules and norms of behavior that govern relationships and promote order and harmony in a society or community

Social psychology: branch of psychology that studies how the thoughts and feelings of individuals are influenced in social situations and how the presence of others can shape individual behaviors

Stereotype: an oversimplified idea (often untrue or unfair) of how people or things are, based on a particular characteristic.

Traits: habitual patterns of behavior, thought, and emotion that can be organized into characteristics that meaningfully describe a person. Psychologists using a trait approach to study personality typically view traits as relatively stable over time. They assume there are significant individual differences in these traits, and that traits influence behavior. Allport increasingly preferred an approach that involves studying individuals in detail, rather than studying mean-level tendencies in a sample or population.

World War II (1939–45): global war between the vast majority of world states, including all the great powers of the time.

PEOPLE MENTIONED IN THE TEXT

Theodor Adorno (1903–69) was a German sociologist, known for his critical theory of society.

Floyd Henry Allport (1890–1979) was a founder of both experimental social psychology and personality psychology, and the elder brother of Gordon Allport.

Jerome Bruner (b. 1915) is a cognitive, developmental, and educational psychologist. In the earlier stages of his career, he was instrumental in developing modern cognitive psychology, in which he challenged psychologists to study people's internal interpretations and cognitions of events.

Joshua Correll is an American social psychologist at the University of Colorado, Boulder.

Patricia Devine is an American social psychologist best known for her work on automatic, unconscious prejudice.

Frank Dobbin is an American economic sociologist teaching at Harvard University.

John Dovidio is an American social psychologist most known for his work on "aversive racism"—a theory that people are often aware of their own prejudices and social norms but, because they deem these prejudices unacceptable, are often uncomfortable in interracial settings.

Jennifer Eberhardt (b. 1965) is an American social psychologist at Stanford University.

Susan Fiske (b. 1952) is an American social psychologist most known for her work on sexism and gender discrimination.

Sigmund Freud (1856–1939) was an Austrian neurologist and psychologist, the founder of psychoanalysis.

Peter Glick (b. 1956) is an American social psychologist best known for his work on sexism and gender discrimination.

Adolf Hitler (1889–1945) was leader of Germany as chancellor and then dictator from 1933 to 1945.

Irwin Katz is a social and political psychologist most known for his work on ambivalent racism—the idea that people have both positive and negative attitudes toward an out-group.

Diane M. Mackie is an American social psychologist at the University of California, Santa Barbara.

Hugo Münsterberg (1863–1916) was a German-American psychologist who pioneered the application of psychology in the study of industrial settings. His theories offered insights for the management of industrial organizations by explaining the psychological dimension of issues such as employee motivation and job performance.

Benjamin Pasamanick (1915–96) was an American psychiatrist who studied the development of infants.

Thomas Pettigrew is a American social psychologist and former PhD student of Gordon Allport.

Franklin Delano Roosevelt (1882–1945) was president of the United States for three terms (1932–45). Beyond serving as president during World War II, Roosevelt is known for implementing several social and government services and programs, including the Fair Employment Practices Committee.

Laurie Rudman is an American social psychologist best known for her work on the psychology of gender.

Muzafer Sherif (1906–88) was a Turkish-American psychologist who is considered a founder of the field of social psychology. He is particularly noted for his theories on the social judgment—the means by which individuals accept or reject ideas in accordance with social norms—and also for his theories on the causes of prejudice and intergroup conflict within societies.

B. F. Skinner (1904–90) was an American psychologist, philosopher, and author, one of the founders of psychological behaviorism.

Eliot R. Smith is an American social psychologist at Indiana University.

Cookie White Stephan is a sociologist and retired faculty member at New Mexico State University.

Walter G. Stephan is a social psychologist and emeritus professor at New Mexico State University.

William Stern (1871–1938) was a Gestalt personality psychologist who believed in the "unity" of the personality system—i.e. personality cannot accurately be described as the sum of a person's traits; instead, the combination of each person's traits creates a unique profile or individuality.

Henri Tajfel (1919–82) was a British social psychologist known for his work on prejudice and identity.

George Zipf (1902–50) was an American linguist who gave his name to Zipf's Law on word frequency.

WORKS CITED

WORKS CITED

Akhtar, Salman, and Mary Kay O'Neil, eds. *On Freud's "Beyond the Pleasure Principle."* London: Karnac Books, 2011.

Allport, G. W. "Gordon W. Allport." In *History of Psychology in Autobiography*, edited by E. Boring and G. Lindsay, vol. 5, 1–25. New York: Appleton-Century-Crofts, 1967.

The Nature of Prejudice. New York: Basic Books, 1979.

Personality: A Psychological Interpretation. New York: Henry Holt, 1937.

Cleburne v. Cleburne Living Center, Inc., 473 US 432—Supreme Court 1985, 464.

Crocker, Jennifer, and Brenda Major. "Social Stigma and Self-Esteem: The Self-Protective Properties of Stigma." *Psychological Review* 96, no. 4 (1989): 608–30.

Devine, Patricia G. "Stereotypes and Prejudice: Their Automatic and Controlled Components." *Journal of Personality and Social Psychology* 56, no. 1 (1989): 5–18.

Dovidio, John F., Peter Glick, and Laurie A. Rudman. "Introduction: Reflecting on *The Nature of Prejudice*: Fifty Years after Allport." In *On the Nature of Prejudice: Fifty Years after Allport*, 1–15. New York: Wiley, 2005.

On the Nature of Prejudice: Fifty Years after Allport. Abingdon: Blackwell Publishing, 2005.

Elms, Alan C. *Uncovering Lives: The Uneasy Alliance of Biography and Psychology.* Oxford: Oxford University Press, 1994, 79–80.

Haggbloom, Steven J., Renee Warnick, Jason E. Warnick, Vinessa K. Jones, Gary L. Yarbrough, Tenea M. Russell, Chris M. Borecky, Reagan McGahhey, John L. Powell, Jamie Beavers, and Emmanuelle Monte. "The 100 Most Eminent Psychologists of the 20th Century." *Review of General Psychology* 6, no. 2 (2002): 139–52.

Herek, Gregory M. "Religious Orientation and Prejudice: A Comparison of Racial and Sexual Attitudes." *Personality and Social Psychology Bulletin* 13, no. 1 (1987): 34–44.

Hjelle, L. A., and D. J. Ziegler. *Personality Theories: Basic Assumptions, Research, and Applications.* New York: McGraw-Hill, 1992.

Katz, Irwin. "Gordon Allport's *The Nature of Prejudice*." *Political Psychology* 12, no. 1 (1991): 125–57.

Nicholson, Ian A. M. *Inventing Personality: Gordon Allport and the Science of Selfhood*. Washington, DC: American Psychological Association, 2003.

Pasamanick, Benjamin. "A Comparative Study of the Behavioral Development of Negro Infants." *The Pedagogical Seminary and Journal of Genetic Psychology* 69, no. 1 (1946): 3–44.

Pettigrew, Thomas. Preface to *The Nature of Prejudice*, by John F. Dovidio, Peter Glick, and Laurie A. Rudman. New York: Basic Books, 1979.

Pettigrew, Thomas F. "Gordon Willard Allport: A Tribute." *Journal of Social Issues* 55, no. 3 (1999): 415–28.

Pettigrew, Thomas F., and Linda R. Tropp. "A Meta-analytic Test of Intergroup Contact Theory." *Journal of Personality and Social Psychology* 90, no. 5 (2006): 751–83.

Skinner, Burrhus Frederic. *About Behaviorism*. New York: Random House, 2011.

Zipf, George. *Human Behavior and the Principle of Least Effort: An Introduction to Human Ecology*. Cambridge, MA: Addison-Wesley, 1949.

Zirkel, Sabrina, and Nancy Cantor. "50 Years after Brown v. Board of Education: The Promise and Challenge of Multicultural Education." *Journal of Social Issues* 60, no. 1 (2004): 1–15.

THE MACAT LIBRARY
BY DISCIPLINE

AFRICANA STUDIES

Chinua Achebe's *An Image of Africa: Racism in Conrad's Heart of Darkness*
W. E. B. Du Bois's *The Souls of Black Folk*
Zora Neale Huston's *Characteristics of Negro Expression*
Martin Luther King Jr's *Why We Can't Wait*
Toni Morrison's *Playing in the Dark: Whiteness in the American Literary Imagination*

ANTHROPOLOGY

Arjun Appadurai's *Modernity at Large: Cultural Dimensions of Globalisation*
Philippe Ariès's *Centuries of Childhood*
Franz Boas's *Race, Language and Culture*
Kim Chan & Renée Mauborgne's *Blue Ocean Strategy*
Jared Diamond's *Guns, Germs & Steel: the Fate of Human Societies*
Jared Diamond's *Collapse: How Societies Choose to Fail or Survive*
E. E. Evans-Pritchard's *Witchcraft, Oracles and Magic Among the Azande*
James Ferguson's *The Anti-Politics Machine*
Clifford Geertz's *The Interpretation of Cultures*
David Graeber's *Debt: the First 5000 Years*
Karen Ho's *Liquidated: An Ethnography of Wall Street*
Geert Hofstede's *Culture's Consequences: Comparing Values, Behaviors, Institutes and Organizations across Nations*
Claude Lévi-Strauss's *Structural Anthropology*
Jay Macleod's *Ain't No Makin' It: Aspirations and Attainment in a Low-Income Neighborhood*
Saba Mahmood's *The Politics of Piety: The Islamic Revival and the Feminist Subject*
Marcel Mauss's *The Gift*

BUSINESS

Jean Lave & Etienne Wenger's *Situated Learning*
Theodore Levitt's *Marketing Myopia*
Burton G. Malkiel's *A Random Walk Down Wall Street*
Douglas McGregor's *The Human Side of Enterprise*
Michael Porter's *Competitive Strategy: Creating and Sustaining Superior Performance*
John Kotter's *Leading Change*
C. K. Prahalad & Gary Hamel's *The Core Competence of the Corporation*

CRIMINOLOGY

Michelle Alexander's *The New Jim Crow: Mass Incarceration in the Age of Colorblindness*
Michael R. Gottfredson & Travis Hirschi's *A General Theory of Crime*
Richard Herrnstein & Charles A. Murray's *The Bell Curve: Intelligence and Class Structure in American Life*
Elizabeth Loftus's *Eyewitness Testimony*
Jay Macleod's *Ain't No Makin' It: Aspirations and Attainment in a Low-Income Neighborhood*
Philip Zimbardo's *The Lucifer Effect*

ECONOMICS

Janet Abu-Lughod's *Before European Hegemony*
Ha-Joon Chang's *Kicking Away the Ladder*
David Brion Davis's *The Problem of Slavery in the Age of Revolution*
Milton Friedman's *The Role of Monetary Policy*
Milton Friedman's *Capitalism and Freedom*
David Graeber's *Debt: the First 5000 Years*
Friedrich Hayek's *The Road to Serfdom*
Karen Ho's *Liquidated: An Ethnography of Wall Street*

John Maynard Keynes's *The General Theory of Employment, Interest and Money*
Charles P. Kindleberger's *Manias, Panics and Crashes*
Robert Lucas's *Why Doesn't Capital Flow from Rich to Poor Countries?*
Burton G. Malkiel's *A Random Walk Down Wall Street*
Thomas Robert Malthus's *An Essay on the Principle of Population*
Karl Marx's *Capital*
Thomas Piketty's *Capital in the Twenty-First Century*
Amartya Sen's *Development as Freedom*
Adam Smith's *The Wealth of Nations*
Nassim Nicholas Taleb's *The Black Swan: The Impact of the Highly Improbable*
Amos Tversky's & Daniel Kahneman's *Judgment under Uncertainty: Heuristics and Biases*
Mahbub Ul Haq's *Reflections on Human Development*
Max Weber's *The Protestant Ethic and the Spirit of Capitalism*

FEMINISM AND GENDER STUDIES

Judith Butler's *Gender Trouble*
Simone De Beauvoir's *The Second Sex*
Michel Foucault's *History of Sexuality*
Betty Friedan's *The Feminine Mystique*
Saba Mahmood's *The Politics of Piety: The Islamic Revival and the Feminist Subject*
Joan Wallach Scott's *Gender and the Politics of History*
Mary Wollstonecraft's *A Vindication of the Rights of Woman*
Virginia Woolf's *A Room of One's Own*

GEOGRAPHY

The Brundtland Report's *Our Common Future*
Rachel Carson's *Silent Spring*
Charles Darwin's *On the Origin of Species*
James Ferguson's *The Anti-Politics Machine*
Jane Jacobs's *The Death and Life of Great American Cities*
James Lovelock's *Gaia: A New Look at Life on Earth*
Amartya Sen's *Development as Freedom*
Mathis Wackernagel & William Rees's *Our Ecological Footprint*

HISTORY

Janet Abu-Lughod's *Before European Hegemony*
Benedict Anderson's *Imagined Communities*
Bernard Bailyn's *The Ideological Origins of the American Revolution*
Hanna Batatu's *The Old Social Classes And The Revolutionary Movements Of Iraq*
Christopher Browning's *Ordinary Men: Reserve Police Batallion 101 and the Final Solution in Poland*
Edmund Burke's *Reflections on the Revolution in France*
William Cronon's *Nature's Metropolis: Chicago And The Great West*
Alfred W. Crosby's *The Columbian Exchange*
Hamid Dabashi's *Iran: A People Interrupted*
David Brion Davis's *The Problem of Slavery in the Age of Revolution*
Nathalie Zemon Davis's *The Return of Martin Guerre*
Jared Diamond's *Guns, Germs & Steel: the Fate of Human Societies*
Frank Dikotter's *Mao's Great Famine*
John W Dower's *War Without Mercy: Race And Power In The Pacific War*
W. E. B. Du Bois's *The Souls of Black Folk*
Richard J. Evans's *In Defence of History*
Lucien Febvre's *The Problem of Unbelief in the 16th Century*
Sheila Fitzpatrick's *Everyday Stalinism*

The Macat Library By Discipline

Eric Foner's *Reconstruction: America's Unfinished Revolution, 1863-1877*
Michel Foucault's *Discipline and Punish*
Michel Foucault's *History of Sexuality*
Francis Fukuyama's *The End of History and the Last Man*
John Lewis Gaddis's *We Now Know: Rethinking Cold War History*
Ernest Gellner's *Nations and Nationalism*
Eugene Genovese's *Roll, Jordan, Roll: The World the Slaves Made*
Carlo Ginzburg's *The Night Battles*
Daniel Goldhagen's *Hitler's Willing Executioners*
Jack Goldstone's *Revolution and Rebellion in the Early Modern World*
Antonio Gramsci's *The Prison Notebooks*
Alexander Hamilton, John Jay & James Madison's *The Federalist Papers*
Christopher Hill's *The World Turned Upside Down*
Carole Hillenbrand's *The Crusades: Islamic Perspectives*
Thomas Hobbes's *Leviathan*
Eric Hobsbawm's *The Age Of Revolution*
John A. Hobson's *Imperialism: A Study*
Albert Hourani's *History of the Arab Peoples*
Samuel P. Huntington's *The Clash of Civilizations and the Remaking of World Order*
C. L. R. James's *The Black Jacobins*
Tony Judt's *Postwar: A History of Europe Since 1945*
Ernst Kantorowicz's *The King's Two Bodies: A Study in Medieval Political Theology*
Paul Kennedy's *The Rise and Fall of the Great Powers*
Ian Kershaw's *The "Hitler Myth": Image and Reality in the Third Reich*
John Maynard Keynes's *The General Theory of Employment, Interest and Money*
Charles P. Kindleberger's *Manias, Panics and Crashes*
Martin Luther King Jr's *Why We Can't Wait*
Henry Kissinger's *World Order: Reflections on the Character of Nations and the Course of History*
Thomas Kuhn's *The Structure of Scientific Revolutions*
Georges Lefebvre's *The Coming of the French Revolution*
John Locke's *Two Treatises of Government*
Niccolò Machiavelli's *The Prince*
Thomas Robert Malthus's *An Essay on the Principle of Population*
Mahmood Mamdani's *Citizen and Subject: Contemporary Africa And The Legacy Of Late Colonialism*
Karl Marx's *Capital*
Stanley Milgram's *Obedience to Authority*
John Stuart Mill's *On Liberty*
Thomas Paine's *Common Sense*
Thomas Paine's *Rights of Man*
Geoffrey Parker's *Global Crisis: War, Climate Change and Catastrophe in the Seventeenth Century*
Jonathan Riley-Smith's *The First Crusade and the Idea of Crusading*
Jean-Jacques Rousseau's *The Social Contract*
Joan Wallach Scott's *Gender and the Politics of History*
Theda Skocpol's *States and Social Revolutions*
Adam Smith's *The Wealth of Nations*
Timothy Snyder's *Bloodlands: Europe Between Hitler and Stalin*
Sun Tzu's *The Art of War*
Keith Thomas's *Religion and the Decline of Magic*
Thucydides's *The History of the Peloponnesian War*
Frederick Jackson Turner's *The Significance of the Frontier in American History*
Odd Arne Westad's *The Global Cold War: Third World Interventions And The Making Of Our Times*

LITERATURE

Chinua Achebe's *An Image of Africa: Racism in Conrad's Heart of Darkness*
Roland Barthes's *Mythologies*
Homi K. Bhabha's *The Location of Culture*
Judith Butler's *Gender Trouble*
Simone De Beauvoir's *The Second Sex*
Ferdinand De Saussure's *Course in General Linguistics*
T. S. Eliot's *The Sacred Wood: Essays on Poetry and Criticism*
Zora Neale Huston's *Characteristics of Negro Expression*
Toni Morrison's *Playing in the Dark: Whiteness in the American Literary Imagination*
Edward Said's *Orientalism*
Gayatri Chakravorty Spivak's *Can the Subaltern Speak?*
Mary Wollstonecraft's *A Vindication of the Rights of Women*
Virginia Woolf's *A Room of One's Own*

PHILOSOPHY

Elizabeth Anscombe's *Modern Moral Philosophy*
Hannah Arendt's *The Human Condition*
Aristotle's *Metaphysics*
Aristotle's *Nicomachean Ethics*
Edmund Gettier's *Is Justified True Belief Knowledge?*
Georg Wilhelm Friedrich Hegel's *Phenomenology of Spirit*
David Hume's *Dialogues Concerning Natural Religion*
David Hume's *The Enquiry for Human Understanding*
Immanuel Kant's *Religion within the Boundaries of Mere Reason*
Immanuel Kant's *Critique of Pure Reason*
Søren Kierkegaard's *The Sickness Unto Death*
Søren Kierkegaard's *Fear and Trembling*
C. S. Lewis's *The Abolition of Man*
Alasdair MacIntyre's *After Virtue*
Marcus Aurelius's *Meditations*
Friedrich Nietzsche's *On the Genealogy of Morality*
Friedrich Nietzsche's *Beyond Good and Evil*
Plato's *Republic*
Plato's *Symposium*
Jean-Jacques Rousseau's *The Social Contract*
Gilbert Ryle's *The Concept of Mind*
Baruch Spinoza's *Ethics*
Sun Tzu's *The Art of War*
Ludwig Wittgenstein's *Philosophical Investigations*

POLITICS

Benedict Anderson's *Imagined Communities*
Aristotle's *Politics*
Bernard Bailyn's *The Ideological Origins of the American Revolution*
Edmund Burke's *Reflections on the Revolution in France*
John C. Calhoun's *A Disquisition on Government*
Ha-Joon Chang's *Kicking Away the Ladder*
Hamid Dabashi's *Iran: A People Interrupted*
Hamid Dabashi's *Theology of Discontent: The Ideological Foundation of the Islamic Revolution in Iran*
Robert Dahl's *Democracy and its Critics*
Robert Dahl's *Who Governs?*
David Brion Davis's *The Problem of Slavery in the Age of Revolution*

Alexis De Tocqueville's *Democracy in America*
James Ferguson's *The Anti-Politics Machine*
Frank Dikotter's *Mao's Great Famine*
Sheila Fitzpatrick's *Everyday Stalinism*
Eric Foner's *Reconstruction: America's Unfinished Revolution, 1863-1877*
Milton Friedman's *Capitalism and Freedom*
Francis Fukuyama's *The End of History and the Last Man*
John Lewis Gaddis's *We Now Know: Rethinking Cold War History*
Ernest Gellner's *Nations and Nationalism*
David Graeber's *Debt: the First 5000 Years*
Antonio Gramsci's *The Prison Notebooks*
Alexander Hamilton, John Jay & James Madison's *The Federalist Papers*
Friedrich Hayek's *The Road to Serfdom*
Christopher Hill's *The World Turned Upside Down*
Thomas Hobbes's *Leviathan*
John A. Hobson's *Imperialism: A Study*
Samuel P. Huntington's *The Clash of Civilizations and the Remaking of World Order*
Tony Judt's *Postwar: A History of Europe Since 1945*
David C. Kang's *China Rising: Peace, Power and Order in East Asia*
Paul Kennedy's *The Rise and Fall of Great Powers*
Robert Keohane's *After Hegemony*
Martin Luther King Jr.'s *Why We Can't Wait*
Henry Kissinger's *World Order: Reflections on the Character of Nations and the Course of History*
John Locke's *Two Treatises of Government*
Niccolò Machiavelli's *The Prince*
Thomas Robert Malthus's *An Essay on the Principle of Population*
Mahmood Mamdani's *Citizen and Subject: Contemporary Africa And The Legacy Of Late Colonialism*
Karl Marx's *Capital*
John Stuart Mill's *On Liberty*
John Stuart Mill's *Utilitarianism*
Hans Morgenthau's *Politics Among Nations*
Thomas Paine's *Common Sense*
Thomas Paine's *Rights of Man*
Thomas Piketty's *Capital in the Twenty-First Century*
Robert D. Putman's *Bowling Alone*
John Rawls's *Theory of Justice*
Jean-Jacques Rousseau's *The Social Contract*
Theda Skocpol's *States and Social Revolutions*
Adam Smith's *The Wealth of Nations*
Sun Tzu's *The Art of War*
Henry David Thoreau's *Civil Disobedience*
Thucydides's *The History of the Peloponnesian War*
Kenneth Waltz's *Theory of International Politics*
Max Weber's *Politics as a Vocation*
Odd Arne Westad's *The Global Cold War: Third World Interventions And The Making Of Our Times*

POSTCOLONIAL STUDIES

Roland Barthes's *Mythologies*
Frantz Fanon's *Black Skin, White Masks*
Homi K. Bhabha's *The Location of Culture*
Gustavo Gutiérrez's *A Theology of Liberation*
Edward Said's *Orientalism*
Gayatri Chakravorty Spivak's *Can the Subaltern Speak?*

PSYCHOLOGY

Gordon Allport's *The Nature of Prejudice*
Alan Baddeley & Graham Hitch's *Aggression: A Social Learning Analysis*
Albert Bandura's *Aggression: A Social Learning Analysis*
Leon Festinger's *A Theory of Cognitive Dissonance*
Sigmund Freud's *The Interpretation of Dreams*
Betty Friedan's *The Feminine Mystique*
Michael R. Gottfredson & Travis Hirschi's *A General Theory of Crime*
Eric Hoffer's *The True Believer: Thoughts on the Nature of Mass Movements*
William James's *Principles of Psychology*
Elizabeth Loftus's *Eyewitness Testimony*
A. H. Maslow's *A Theory of Human Motivation*
Stanley Milgram's *Obedience to Authority*
Steven Pinker's *The Better Angels of Our Nature*
Oliver Sacks's *The Man Who Mistook His Wife For a Hat*
Richard Thaler & Cass Sunstein's *Nudge: Improving Decisions About Health, Wealth and Happiness*
Amos Tversky's *Judgment under Uncertainty: Heuristics and Biases*
Philip Zimbardo's *The Lucifer Effect*

SCIENCE

Rachel Carson's *Silent Spring*
William Cronon's *Nature's Metropolis: Chicago And The Great West*
Alfred W. Crosby's *The Columbian Exchange*
Charles Darwin's *On the Origin of Species*
Richard Dawkin's *The Selfish Gene*
Thomas Kuhn's *The Structure of Scientific Revolutions*
Geoffrey Parker's *Global Crisis: War, Climate Change and Catastrophe in the Seventeenth Century*
Mathis Wackernagel & William Rees's *Our Ecological Footprint*

SOCIOLOGY

Michelle Alexander's *The New Jim Crow: Mass Incarceration in the Age of Colorblindness*
Gordon Allport's *The Nature of Prejudice*
Albert Bandura's *Aggression: A Social Learning Analysis*
Hanna Batatu's *The Old Social Classes And The Revolutionary Movements Of Iraq*
Ha-Joon Chang's *Kicking Away the Ladder*
W. E. B. Du Bois's *The Souls of Black Folk*
Émile Durkheim's *On Suicide*
Frantz Fanon's *Black Skin, White Masks*
Frantz Fanon's *The Wretched of the Earth*
Eric Foner's *Reconstruction: America's Unfinished Revolution, 1863-1877*
Eugene Genovese's *Roll, Jordan, Roll: The World the Slaves Made*
Jack Goldstone's *Revolution and Rebellion in the Early Modern World*
Antonio Gramsci's *The Prison Notebooks*
Richard Herrnstein & Charles A Murray's *The Bell Curve: Intelligence and Class Structure in American Life*
Eric Hoffer's *The True Believer: Thoughts on the Nature of Mass Movements*
Jane Jacobs's *The Death and Life of Great American Cities*
Robert Lucas's *Why Doesn't Capital Flow from Rich to Poor Countries?*
Jay Macleod's *Ain't No Makin' It: Aspirations and Attainment in a Low Income Neighborhood*
Elaine May's *Homeward Bound: American Families in the Cold War Era*
Douglas McGregor's *The Human Side of Enterprise*
C. Wright Mills's *The Sociological Imagination*

The Macat Library By Discipline

Thomas Piketty's *Capital in the Twenty-First Century*
Robert D. Putman's *Bowling Alone*
David Riesman's *The Lonely Crowd: A Study of the Changing American Character*
Edward Said's *Orientalism*
Joan Wallach Scott's *Gender and the Politics of History*
Theda Skocpol's *States and Social Revolutions*
Max Weber's *The Protestant Ethic and the Spirit of Capitalism*

THEOLOGY

Augustine's *Confessions*
Benedict's *Rule of St Benedict*
Gustavo Gutiérrez's *A Theology of Liberation*
Carole Hillenbrand's *The Crusades: Islamic Perspectives*
David Hume's *Dialogues Concerning Natural Religion*
Immanuel Kant's *Religion within the Boundaries of Mere Reason*
Ernst Kantorowicz's *The King's Two Bodies: A Study in Medieval Political Theology*
Søren Kierkegaard's *The Sickness Unto Death*
C. S. Lewis's *The Abolition of Man*
Saba Mahmood's *The Politics of Piety: The Islamic Revival and the Feminist Subject*
Baruch Spinoza's *Ethics*
Keith Thomas's *Religion and the Decline of Magic*

COMING SOON

Chris Argyris's *The Individual and the Organisation*
Seyla Benhabib's *The Rights of Others*
Walter Benjamin's *The Work Of Art in the Age of Mechanical Reproduction*
John Berger's *Ways of Seeing*
Pierre Bourdieu's *Outline of a Theory of Practice*
Mary Douglas's *Purity and Danger*
Roland Dworkin's *Taking Rights Seriously*
James G. March's *Exploration and Exploitation in Organisational Learning*
Ikujiro Nonaka's *A Dynamic Theory of Organizational Knowledge Creation*
Griselda Pollock's *Vision and Difference*
Amartya Sen's *Inequality Re-Examined*
Susan Sontag's *On Photography*
Yasser Tabbaa's *The Transformation of Islamic Art*
Ludwig von Mises's *Theory of Money and Credit*

Macat Disciplines

Access the greatest ideas and thinkers across entire disciplines, including

MAN AND THE ENVIRONMENT

The Brundtland Report's, *Our Common Future*
Rachel Carson's, *Silent Spring*
James Lovelock's, *Gaia: A New Look at Life on Earth*
Mathis Wackernagel & William Rees's, *Our Ecological Footprint*

Macat analyses are available from all good bookshops and libraries.

Access hundreds of analyses through one, multimedia tool.
Join free for one month **library.macat.com**

Macat Pairs

Analyse historical and modern issues from opposite sides of an argument. Pairs include:

ARE WE FUNDAMENTALLY GOOD - OR BAD?

Steven Pinker's
The Better Angels of Our Nature

Stephen Pinker's gloriously optimistic 2011 book argues that, despite humanity's biological tendency toward violence, we are, in fact, less violent today than ever before. To prove his case, Pinker lays out pages of detailed statistical evidence. For him, much of the credit for the decline goes to the eighteenth-century Enlightenment movement, whose ideas of liberty, tolerance, and respect for the value of human life filtered down through society and affected how people thought. That psychological change led to behavioral change—and overall we became more peaceful. Critics countered that humanity could never overcome the biological urge toward violence; others argued that Pinker's statistics were flawed.

Philip Zimbardo's
The Lucifer Effect

Some psychologists believe those who commit cruelty are innately evil. Zimbardo disagrees. In *The Lucifer Effect*, he argues that sometimes good people do evil things simply because of the situations they find themselves in, citing many historical examples to illustrate his point. Zimbardo details his 1971 Stanford prison experiment, where ordinary volunteers playing guards in a mock prison rapidly became abusive. But he also describes the tortures committed by US army personnel in Iraq's Abu Ghraib prison in 2003—and how he himself testified in defence of one of those guards. committed by US army personnel in Iraq's Abu Ghraib prison in 2003—and how he himself testified in defence of one of those guards.

Macat analyses are available from all good bookshops and libraries.

Access hundreds of analyses through one, multimedia tool.

Join free for one month **library.macat.com**

MACAT

Macat Pairs
*Analyse historical and modern issues
from opposite sides of an argument.
Pairs include:*

MACAT

HOW WE RELATE TO EACH OTHER AND SOCIETY

Jean-Jacques Rousseau's
The Social Contract

Rousseau's famous work sets out the radical concept of the 'social contract': a give-and-take relationship between individual freedom and social order.

If people are free to do as they like, governed only by their own sense of justice, they are also vulnerable to chaos and violence. To avoid this, Rousseau proposes, they should agree to give up some freedom to benefit from the protection of social and political organization. But this deal is only just if societies are led by the collective needs and desires of the people, and able to control the private interests of individuals. For Rousseau, the only legitimate form of government is rule by the people.

Robert D. Putnam's
Bowling Alone

In *Bowling Alone*, Robert Putnam argues that Americans have become disconnected from one another and from the institutions of their common life, and investigates the consequences of this change.

Looking at a range of indicators, from membership in formal organizations to the number of invitations being extended to informal dinner parties, Putnam demonstrates that Americans are interacting less and creating less "social capital" – with potentially disastrous implications for their society.

It would be difficult to overstate the impact of *Bowling Alone*, one of the most frequently cited social science publications of the last half-century.

Macat analyses are available from all good bookshops and libraries.